GODS
LAST WILL AND TESTAMENT

Gods Last Will and Testament

Interior Book Design and Layout by
www.integrativeink.com

ISBN: 978-0-9826092-0-0

MERRY CHRISTMAS

My Dearest (2nd Wife),

I pray this finds all of your Loved ones well. I am so happy for you that you have found a great place in your life with GOD. As I told you in a text, GOD is working in my life as well. It didn't start right away and I began to spiral down with grief and alcohol after our separation. I was so torn. I knew that I had lost my Soul Mate, but I couldn't continue the relationship in its impenetrable state. I tried very hard for you to believe in me again, but I knew you didn't have any respect for me and would never get it back.

I have no regrets about you coming into my life. It was all in the Man-U- “Script”. You had pieces to a puzzle that I would have never discovered had it not been for you. I want to Thank You once again for being a part of my life as painful as it was for you. But you did complete me and my Purpose for GOD. I will be forever grateful for the time we shared.

I received a call from Bill after I had made a complete ass out of myself at a pretty elaborate private function. He didn't chastise me, he confronted me like a true friend should and I was ready to listen this time. This is when I picked up the one thing that has cursed me for the last five years. This was my opportunity to finally complete this and get it off my plate once and for all.

I now know why I had been so reluctant to pick this book project up. I thought putting the website together was hard, this has been the most daunting task I have ever taken on. It's unbelievable the crooks in this industry. Wow, you just can't escape it.

I have said "I am sorry" a thousand times. My behavior was inexcusable and I appreciate all that you did to keep the relationship together. As I read my own words, I realize that I couldn't have put up with me either. LOL

This is the manuscript of my book that is being released in a few weeks. I wanted to send you a hard copy for Christmas, but this is the best that I can do. I hope you enjoy the sneak peek.

I truly pray for you daily. I pray that your life turns out like the dreams you once had. I am so sorry you were robbed the gift of being a child. Life has always fallen on your shoulders.

I Will Forever Love You

Take Care,

Nate

TABLE OF CONTENTS

PREFACE

I would like to dedicate this book to my Creator. He has been with me every step of the way. Without His guidance, my time here on earth would be inconsequential. Just another One Talent consumer that produced more One Talent consumers.

I was moved to create an Earthly Entity for GOD. This is his Last Will and Testament and one side of the Seven Sealed, Two-Sided Scroll. GOD's LEGACY TRUST LLC is where I invested my One Talent. His Temple will rise up with the Bricks of Mankind. Each of us are bricks that can be used for the Glory of GOD or the "Weapons of GOD's Destruction". Our lives are a microcosm of time and ultimately we do become "Dust in the Wind". What will our Generations LEGACY Be?

Before anyone cries out "BLASPHEMY", "CRUCIFY HIM" let me preface that all I do is for Christ. I am merely a humble servant of the Lord and "A Godly Man". I make no visual or audio claims for my Godly encounters, it is what GOD puts on my heart that resounds in my brain. After countless failures and hardships, I was given signs to Endeavor to Persevere.

I have spent years trying to find what exactly IT is, that I am here for. Of course immediate financial requirements took precedence and I entered into the work place (Rat Race) a College Educated, ill equipped young man. I eagerly accepted knowledge that had inadvertently omitted Financial Intelligence. It took me years of scratching in the dirt to reach the bottom and lose everything. I guess in a way, I am very fortunate to hit the bottom. Only at the bottom, could I see the top. The top is CONTENTMENT. How much is enough? This is a question you will have to search your heart for your own set of answers and consequences.

I found my answer through books and GOD, who had only just begun to come into my life. I can only pray to GOD to bless me with a $1 million dollars, but I know that only gives into temptation. I know that if IT is to be, IT is up to me. Now came the hard part, REALLY learning to read at the age of 42. I read countless books, most were Crap. Yet through this re-invention period of my life, I was becoming a completely different man. The focus of my studies were on Financial, Spiritual and Relationships.

The Financial books enlightened me to achieve a vision of Financial Freedom. I got my dream of a condo on the beach and was still discontent with myself. We are all like Rats in the Maze, looking for the next Cheese Station. - Who Moved My Cheese

There has got to be MORE!!!

The Spiritual books were great, but based on FAITH not FACTS. Faith can be very difficult to accept when you are dealing with the potholes of life. I asked my GOD to Bless my Purpose for Him for the five years of Hell I was going through. He was maturing me in Christ and I was not ready to be His Witness. I don't know if I am ready now, but I have my Faith and I have GOD's WORD. I think we all grow and mature in Christ with Time.

I read ALL the Relationship books. I still can't figure women out. LOL Maybe that's why I am now alone. The alone time was a Blessing that enabled me the time to find out who I am, my new name in Christ and my Purpose for GOD. Wow, how many people know all that? It's a Hell of a script. I pray that GOD touches your heart and impacts you in a way that you have never felt before. -Amen

I never thought it could happen to me – The Jerk

THE VESSEL

FIRST SIDE OF THE SEVEN SEALED TWO-SIDED SCROLL

LEGACYWILLANDTRUST.COM

GROWING GOD BACK INTO OUR WORLD
ONE GENERATION AT A TIME

THIS WEBSITE WILL ENABLE YOU TO CREATE YOUR OWN LIVING WILL AND TRUST FREE OF CHARGE.

AFTER A SERIES OF QUESTIONS, YOU MAY PRINT YOUR DOCUMENT, HAVE YOUR SIGNATURE NOTARIZED AND FILE PROPERLY.

YOU WILL BE ABLE TO DETERMINE WHO WILL MAKE LIFE SUSTAINING DECISIONS ON YOUR BEHALF,

HANDLE YOUR FINAL AFFAIRS WITH YOUR IMMEDIATE LOVED ONES

AND DIRECT THE REST OF YOUR WORLDLY POSSESSIONS TO ALL OF YOUR HEIRS, COUNTRY, CHARITIES, PASSIONS AND GOD.

THE LEGACY YOU LEAVE ON THIS EARTH WILL YIELD FRUIT TO THE BENEFACTORS OF YOUR CHOICE FOR AN ETERNITY.

YOUR ORIGINAL INVESTMENT WILL NEVER BE TOUCHED.

A PERCENTAGE OF YOUR YIELD WILL BE RE-INVESTED AND THE REMAINDER TO BE DISBURSED AT YOUR DIRECTION.

YOUR BENEFACTORS WILL RECEIVE DIVIDEND CHECKS FROM YOUR LIMITED LIABILITY CORPORATION THAT IS NAMED BY YOU.

THE NAME OF THIS LLC IS WHAT WILL BE PRINTED ON EVERY LEGACY CHECK DISBURSED TO ALL OF YOUR LOVED ONES FOR AN ETERNITY.

BE CREATIVE AND LET THE WORLD KNOW YOUR WERE HERE AND LEFT YOUR MARK WITH A LEGACY.

THE LEGACY THAT YOU LEAVE TO ALL FUTURE GENERATIONS OF YOUR BLOODLINE WILL BE SUBJECT TO A GOVERNMENTAL TAX.

I PRAY THAT OUR GOVERNMENT WILL MAKE IT MODEST AND USE THIS NEW FOUND TAXABLE INCOME STREAM TO RE-BUILD SOCIAL SECURITY.

THE LEGACY THAT YOU LEAVE TO YOUR FAVORITE CHARITIES AND PASSIONS WILL CONTINUALLY BLESS THEM WITH A LEGACY CHECK FROM YOUR LLC FOR AN ETERNITY.

THE LEGACY THAT YOU LEAVE WILL BE INVESTED INTO WHAT EVER ECONOMY YOU DIRECT IT TO, SO IT WILL CREATE JOBS.

THE LEGACY THAT YOU LEAVE FOR GODS LEGACY TRUST LLC WILL PROVIDE BASIC HEALTH CARE TO THE UNINSURED AT NO EXPENSE TO YOUR HEIRS. FOR MORE INFO
WWW.GODSLEGACYTRUST.COM

THE LEGACY THAT YOU WILL BE A PART OF, IS A GENERATION THAT LEFT THE WORLD A BETTER PLACE.

GOD has put onto my heart a Gift.

He wishes me to share it with Mankind.

GOD desires an Earthly Entity through which his
people can praise HIM and He can Bless
them ten fold. For all future generations
and for an Eternity.

- Your Humble Servant Nathan

EXAMPLE OF HOW THE LEGACY WILL AND TRUST CAN WORK IN A PERFECT WORLD WITH ILLUSTRATIVE BENEFITS

TOTAL BENEFIT - $1 MILLION
YEAR STARTED - 1985
ANNUAL INTEREST YIELDED – 10 %

YEAR	BALANCE	DISBURSED	TAX	CHARITIES	HEIRS
1986	1050000	50000	7500	5000	37500
1987	1102500	5125	8268	5512	41343
1988	1157625	57881	8682	5788	43410
1989	1215506	60775	9116	6077	45581
1990	1276281	63814	9572	6381	47860
1991	1340095	67004	10050	6700	50253
1992	1407100	70355	10553	7035	52766
1993	1477455	73872	11080	7387	55404
1994	1551327	77566	11634	7756	58174
1995	1628894	81444	12216	8144	61083
1996	1710338	85516	12827	8551	64137
1997	1795855	89792	13468	8979	67344
1998	1885648	94282	14142	9428	70711
1999	1979930	98996	14849	9899	74247
2000	2078927	103946	15591	10394	77959

RULE OF 72'S 72/5 = 14.4 YEARS
OUR PRINCIPLE BALANCE HAS DOUBLED

YEAR	BALANCE	DISBURSED	TAX	CHARITIES	HEIRS
2001	2182873	109143	16371	10914	81857
2002	2292017	114600	17190	11460	85950
2003	2406618	120330	18049	12033	90248
2004	2526949	126347	18952	12634	94760
2005	2653296	132664	19899	13266	99498
2006	2785961	139298	20894	13929	104473
2007	2925259	146262	21939	14626	109697
2008	3071522	153576	23036	15357	115182

$2,172,598 $325,889 $217,259 $1,629,448

IF IN 1985 $1 MILLION WAS PUT INTO A LEGACY WILL AND TRUST, THE PRINCIPLE BALANCE WOULD BE $3,071,522.

TOTAL DISBURSEMENTS WOULD HAVE BEEN $2,171,598.

THE GOVERNMENT WOULD HAVE COLLECTED $325,889 BASED ON A TAX RATE OF 15 %. CHARITIES $217,259 BASED ON 10% AND THE HEIRS WOULD HAVE SHARED A TOTAL OF $1,629,448.

THE 2008 DISBURSEMENTS WOULD BE: GOVERNMENT $23,036 – CHARITIES $15,357 AND HEIRS $115,182.

RULES AND REGULATIONS FOR MEMBERS AND CHARITABLE ORGANIZATIONS

---

*EACH MEMBER IS ENTITLED TO AN EQUAL VARIABLE SHARE OF DISBURSEMENTS AT AGE 18.

*MEMBERS MUST REGISTER WITH INVESTMENT BROKER 30 DAYS PRIOR TO EACH BIRTHDAY WITH PROOF OF LINEAGE AND BIRTH CERTIFICATE

*ORGANIZATIONS THAT FAIL TO REGISTER ANNUALLY WILL BE DELETED AND PROCEEDS TO GO INTO MEMBER PROCEEDS

*NO LIENS MAY BE ATTACHED

*NO BACK PAYMENTS

*IF INVESTMENT BROKER FEES ARE EXCESSIVE OR THE RATE OF RETURN FALLS BELOW 10 % FOR 2 YEARS IN THE LAST 5 YEARS A MAJORITY VOTE OF MEMBERS MAY CHANGE INVESTMENT BROKERS TO A DIFFERENT LEGITIMATE BROKER UNDER PRE-SET GUIDELINES. TIE NO CHANGE

*MINIMUM LEGACY CHECK IS $100 AFTER FEES AND EXPENSES, OTHERWISE ACCOUNT WILL RE-INVEST 100 % UNTIL THIS CAN OCCUR

*ONLY DIRECT BLOODLINE LINEAGE QUALIFIES, NO EXTENDED FAMILIES

*SPOUSE OF MEMBER DOES QUALIFY AS MY REPLACEMENT UPON MY DEATH

*MUST REGISTER ALL BIRTHS OF YOUR BLOODLINE WITHIN FIRST YEAR. INCOME STREAM MAY NOT BE SOLD FOR ONE LUMP SUM. BOTH OF THESE INFRACTIONS RISK LOSING YOUR SHARES AT A MAJORITY VOTE. TIE NO

*FUND MUST HAVE A POSITIVE YIELD OR THERE WILL BE NO LEGACY CHECK FOR THAT PERIOD

*IF NO HEIRS OR CHARITIES, DIRECT MY LEGACY TO GODS LEGACY TRUST LLC YES

THE LAMB

SECOND SIDE OF THE SEVEN SEALED TWO-SIDED SCROLL

GOD'S LEGACY TRUST LLC

"ENDEAVOR TO PERSEVERE"

LORD, HOW WILL YOUR ENTITY HEAL THE SICK?

"MOVE THAT BUS" FOR COMMUNITY HEALTH CARE CENTERS. FIND DONORS OF BUILDINGS THAT CAN BE RENOVATED TO ACCOMODATE A MODEST HEALTH CARE CENTER. THE DONORS OF THIS CHARITABLE GIFT WILL HAVE A PLAQUE RECOGNIZING THEIR LEGACY TO THEIR COMMUNITY AND GOD.

THESE CENTERS WILL BE DESIGNED FOR GENERAL PRACTITIONERS. THE COMMUNITY WILL RENOVATE THESE BUILDINGS AND A STAFF WILL BE DETERMINED BY THE NEEDS AND ACCOMODATIONS. THE STAFF PAYROLL AND INSURANCE WILL BE PAID BY GODS LEGACY TRUST LLC VIA A DIVIDEND CHECK INTO THE LLC CREATED BY THE CENTER/DONOR. ALL VARIABLE EXPENSES TO BE PAID BY VOLUNTEER CO-PAYS AND CHARITABLE GIFTS TO THE CENTERS.

THESE CENTERS WILL HAVE AN ARBITRATION AGREEMENT SIGNED BY ALL THAT WISH TO USE THE CENTER. THEY WILL AGREE TO A $250,000 CAP ON LITIGATION PAYOUTS. THE PLANTIFF IS RESPONSIBLE FOR ALL OF THEIR OWN LEGAL EXPENSES IF THEIR SUIT DOES NOT WIN BEFORE AN ARBITRATOR.

THE ONLY EFFECT THAT THESE CENTERS WILL HAVE ON SOMEONE THAT PRESENTLY MAINTAINS THEIR OWN HEALTH INSURANCE IS SHORTER WAITS, LESS TAXES AND THE GRATIFICATION THAT THE UNINSURED IS RECEIVING HEALTH CARE. NO ONE NEED EVER HURT AGAIN AND BE HELPLESS. GOD LOVES AND HEALS HIS PEOPLE.

THE FINANCIAL RECORDS OF GODS LEGACY TRUST LLC AND EACH LLC THAT RECEIVES DIVIDENDS, WILL BE ACCESSIBLE THROUGH PUBLIC RECORDS. THE FINANCIAL PLANNER FOR GODS LEGACY TRUST LLC AND THE LLC'S THEMSELVES WILL POST THEM TO THE WEB.

EVERYONE THAT RECEIVES A DIVIDEND CHECK FROM GODS LEGACY TRUST LLC, QUALIFIES AS A MEMBER AND IS ENTITLED TO ONE VOTE. AT THE TIME OF MY DEATH, CONTROL OF GODS LEGACY TRUST LLC BECOMES THE RESPONSIBILITY OF ALL MEMBERS TO ENSURE THE SURVIVAL OF GODS LEGACY TRUST LLC.

YOU MIGHT ASK YOURSELF, WHAT AM I GETTING OUT OF THIS?

FIRST: I AM FULFILLING MY PURPOSE FOR GOD. THAT WOULD BE A GRATIFICATION THAT COULD NOT BE ARTICULATED ONLY EXPERIENCED.

SECOND: I AM LOOKING OUT FOR THE FUTURE OF MY HEIRS, COUNTRY AND MANKIND.

THIRD: REVENUE FROM THE CONCESSION STAND WILL BE DIVIDED ACCORDINGLY:

"GODS LEGACY TRUST LLC" 90% ,

"FROM THE ESTATE OF NATHAN J. ISBELL - ENDEAVOR TO PERSEVERE" 10%.

YEAH, YOU GUESSED IT. I HAVE A BOOK AND SOME COOL T-SHIRT IDEAS. LOL

I PRAY TO YOU FATHER THAT MY VISION FOR YOU, BY YOU WILL SATISFY YOUR DESIRE FOR AN EARTHLY ENTITY TO HEAL YOUR PEOPLE. NOT A HOUSE MADE OF CEDAR, BUT AN ENTITY AND IDENTITY THAT ALL YOUR CHILDREN WILL REJOICE IN YOUR NAME AND COME TO KNOW THE ONLY WAY TO THE FATHER IS THROUGH HIS SON JESUS CHRIST. THE ONLY MANGOD TO EVER GRACE OUR HUMBLE EXISTENCE BY GIVING HIS OWN LIFE FOR THE SINS OF MANKIND.

THANK YOU FATHER FOR ALL OF YOUR WONDERFUL GIFTS THAT WE MAY HAVE LOST SIGHT OF AND TAKEN FOR GRANTED. LET THIS GIFT OF YOURS TO US, BE AN AWAKENING THAT JESUS LIVES IN US ALL.

AMEN - YOUR HUMBLE SERVANT NATHAN

GODS HEALTHCARE CENTER RULES

1. BE PATIENT TO BE A PATIENT

2. BE RESPECTFUL TO THE PHYSICIAN, NURSE, STAFF AND GOD, THIS IS HIS HOUSE. WE RESERVE THE RIGHT TO REFUSE SERVICE. DON'T SHOW YOUR ASS.

3. FAST LEARN RULE # 1 AND RULE #2. LOL -THE KARATE KID

4. PAY WHAT YOU CAN FOR SERVICES RENDERED. GODS HEALTH CENTERS SURVIVE ON GODS LEGACY TRUST LLC, VOLUNTEER CO-PAYS AND CHARITABLE GIFTS.

5. DON'T ASK WHAT GODS LEGACY TRUST CAN DO FOR YOU, BUT WHAT YOU CAN DO FOR GOD.

6. ALL PATIENTS MUST SIGN AN ARBITRATION AGREEMENT.

7. ALL PATIENTS MUST SIGN A COMPLETE UNDERSTANDING OF WHAT ARBITRATION IS STATEMENT.

8. PATIENTS AGREE IF LITIGATION IS UNAVOIDABLE AND THEIR CASE GOES BEFORE AN ARBITRATOR AND WIN, THE CAP PAYOUT IS $250,000.00 OF WHICH YOUR ATTORNEY WILL GET A LARGE PORTION OF.

9. PATIENTS AGREE IF LITIGATION IS UNAVOIDABLE AND YOU LOSE YOUR CASE BEFORE AN ARBITRATOR, THAT FIRST YOU ARE RESPONSIBLE FOR ALL OF YOUR OWN LEGAL EXPENSES AND UNDERSTAND THAT YOU <u>WILL</u> BE SUED FOR FILING A FRIVOLOUS LAWSUIT. NOW, HOW STRONGLY DO YOU FEEL ABOUT YOUR CASE. 'CAUSE I'M TRYING TO KEEP MY INSURANCE DOWN TO A POINT THAT ONE DAY

GODS LEGACY TRUST HEALTH CARE CENTERS WILL BE SELF INSURED.

10. RESPECT THE FACT THAT EVERYONE HERE IS HURTING AND WAIT YOUR TURN BY SENSE OF URGENCY AND ORDER.

11. DO YOUR PART TO SHARE GODS BLESSINGS WITH OTHER COMMUNITIES.

12. PRAY THAT GOD LOVES YOU SO MUCH, HE GIVES YOU THE GIFT OF HEALTH. LOVE YOUR GOD AS HE LOVES YOU, KNOW THAT HE IS ALWAYS THERE FOR YOU. HE KNOWS YOUR STRUGGLES. REACH OUT TO JESUS CHRIST OUR LORD AND SAVIOR AND HE WILL HEAR YOUR PRAYERS. GOD HEALS HIS CHILDREN.

AMEN - YOUR HUMBLE SERVANT NATHAN

GRACIOUS DONORS OF TIME

PLEASE SEND RESUME AND POSITION YOU ARE CALLED TO DO. THE LORD KNOWS YOU HAVE REQUIREMENTS AND HE WILL PROVIDE.

POSITION
FINANCIAL REQUIREMENT
PREFERRED LOCATION
MOBILITY

PERSONALLY TESTIMONY AS TO WHY YOU WANT TO WORK FOR THE LORD.

LORD, I DON'T THINK THAT THERE IS A GREATER GIFT THAN THE GIFT OF TIME. TIME IS PRECIOUS TO ALL OF US. TIME SPENT FOR THE BETTERMENT OF OTHERS IS A DIRECT HOT-LINE TO THE GOD ALMIGHTY HIMSELF. COME WORK FOR THE LORD BECAUSE YOUR HEART IS LIFTED EVERYTIME YOU MAKE A DIFFERENCE IN SOMEONE ELSES LIFE. THIS GRATIFICATION CAN NOT BE ARTICULATED ONLY EXPERIENCED. THE WAY I FEEL YOUR LOVING PRESENCE FATHER. I WELCOME ALL THAT WOULD SERVE THE LORD. LET IT BE A PRIVILEGE TO SERVE HIS/YOUR PEOPLE.

AMEN - YOUR HUMBLE SERVANT NATHAN

P.S. HURRICANES, TYPHONES, EARTHQUAKES AND FOREST FIRES, OH MY. YOU KNOW THAT FEELING OF HELPING SOMEONE THAT HAS GONE THROUGH ANY OF THE AFOREMENTIONED. IT IS A FEELING THAT YOU SHOULD HAVE EVERYDAY, EVEN WHEN YOU DON'T HEAR ANY APPRECIATION FROM THE HURTING. JESUS HAD A THANKLESS JOB. GET YOUR GOD ON AND THAT WILL BE ALL YOU WILL EVER NEED. HIS LOVE LASTS FOR AN ETERNITY AND YOU WERE/ARE A PART OF IT.

GRACIOUS CASH DONORS

GOD CALLS ON ALL THAT WOULD BE COMPELLED TO RAISE CHARITABLE DONATIONS.

GOD SAYS TITHE TO THE LIVING:

*FAMILY
*CHURCH
*COMMUNITY
*PASSIONS

IN LIFE AND IN DEATH.

GODS ASKS YOU TO REMEMBER HIS LEGACY TO YOU AND LOVE HIM AND HIS PEOPLE AT YOUR DEATH BY LEAVING A LEGACY TO YOUR HEIRS, COUNTRY, CHARITIES, PASSIONS AND HIM.

REMINDER - 90% OF THE PROFITS FROM THE CONCESSION STAND WILL GO TO GODS LEGACY TRUST LLC.

LORD, PLEASE LET EVERYONE UNDERSTAND THAT IT IS WITH YOU THAT WE RECEIVE OUR BLESSINGS. YOU PUT THE SEED IN US. WE PLANT THE SEED AT OUR DEATH, BY INVESTING IN OURSELVES AND GOD. WE ALL HARVEST THE FRUITS OF OUR LIFE LONG LABOR FOR AN ETERNITY.

AMEN - YOUR HUMBLE SERVANT NATHAN

P.S.
THANK YOU

GRACIOUS DONORS OF REAL ESTATE

PLEASE SEND INFO ON YOUR REAL ESTATE THAT YOU WOULD LIKE TO LEAVE AS A LEGACY TO YOUR FAMILY, COMMUNITY AND GOD.

PICTURE
ADDRESS
DETAILS OF PROPERTY:
SQ FT
CONSTRUCTION
OTHER.......

PERSONAL TESTIMONY AS TO WHY YOU THINK YOUR PROPERTY WOULD BE A BETTERMENT FOR YOUR NEIGHBORS AND GOD.

THE NAME THAT YOU WISH TO LEAVE FOR YOUR GRACIOUS GIFT TO MANKIND, SO THAT ALL FUTURE GENERATIONS CAN APPRECIATE YOUR GENEROSITY.
GODS LEGACY TRUST / ______________________LLC.

LORD, PLEASE GIVE LAGNIAPPE (A LITTLE EXTRA) TO THE ONES THAT MAKE YOUR PLAN FOR THEIR OWN LIVES, BETTER FOR THEIR FELLOW MAN. I WOULD HAVE TO SAY THAT THEY HAVE FULFILLED THEIR OWN PURPOSE FOR YOU, FATHER. LET THE HEARTS OF YOUR PEOPLE BE FILLED WITH THE JOY THAT COMES FROM GIVING, FOR THE BETTERMENT OF THEIR NEIGHBOR. LORD, I UNDERSTAND THAT MAINTENANCE WILL BE NEEDED FOR YOUR CENTERS. SHALL I HAVE THE CENTERS POST WHAT THEY NEED ON A MARQUIS AND SEE IF GODS PEOPLE WILL MAKE IT HAPPEN?

AMEN- YOUR HUMBLE SERVANT NATHAN

P.S.
A VERY SPECIAL THANK YOU FROM ME AND YOUR COMMUNITY. WE ALL APPRECIATE YOUR LOVING GODLY HEART.

GRACIOUS CORPORATE SPONSORS

YOU ARE THE LIFE BLOOD TO GODS GIFT. GODS HEALTH CARE CENTERS WILL NEED TO BE RENOVATED TO ACCOMODATE THE NEEDS OF GODS PEOPLE. CHARITABLE DONATIONS MADE TO GODS LEGACY TRUST LLC CAN COME IN THE WAY OF CASH, TIME, SUPPLIES OR PRAYER.

LORD, PLEASE LET THE BUSINESSES THAT PROVIDE BETTERMENT TO EVERYONES LIFE, BE BLESSED AS GODS LEGACY TRUST LLC SOWS ITS SEED INTO EACH AND EVERYONE OF THEM. BLESS US WITH A GREAT HARVEST SO THAT GODS PEOPLE, CAN HELP GODS PEOPLE.

AMEN - YOUR HUMBLE SERVANT NATHAN

P.S.
AS A FORMER STRUGGLING BUSINESS OWNER, I EMPATHIZE WITH YOU. DO WHAT YOU CAN FOR YOUR COMMUNITY, NEIGHBOR AND GOD.

THE QUEST TO FIND MY PURPOSE FOR GOD

First Idea
Monday before Hurricane Ivan hit the Gulf Coast

U-FIX-IT-SHOP

Goal – get started quick before competition has time to react. Set up our monopoly before this idea hits the market. I believe we will see a lot of me too's, but we will have already secured the best locations. We need to look into a way of securing this idea or be in a position to sell franchises.

Idea – you fix it shop with Hydraulic lifts. Coin operated of course, we don't want any labor except have too's. The same concept as a car wash, only at a much higher rate per hour. I don't know how advanced technology has gotten. I don't know all the particulars as of yet, but I believe someone can help us. I think maybe if we could get the machine to take cash or credit card and be able to get a signature or a disclosure that you are on your own.(AS-IS so the speak).

Accessory income – I like this best of all. We get vending machines and sell tools like the cheap Korean packages you get from Sam's Wholesale Club, but we kill them on price. I thought about parts, but you would have to have a reasonably paid person to manage that and I don't want to have any contact with my patrons. I don't want any headaches. The only employee I would have, is a cheap Barney Fife that will make my daily deposit and shut the place down. I think technology should allow me to match receipts to deposits and only alert me when there is a problem.

Property – these lube places are all over. They are a turn key operation after machines are installed. We can survey all the hottest spots and decide how large or small you want to go. We will have all properties submit bids as if we are only interested in one. Then we'll find out what their low is, negotiate down from there and buy all of the ones that are reasonably priced. We keep the good producers and sell off the poor ones.

Problems – customer liability. I don't have a clue, let's hire someone that does. Theft, either Barney is dead or he stole the money. Either way, we are only out one days work. I thought about closing at certain hours, but who the hell am I to tell them when they can work on their own car, on the clock and with tools we sold them. The night shift may require Andy instead of Barney. This problem is a plus. If they strand the car there, we tow it to our salvage yard where we charge the customer a tow and storage fee and we file for a mechanics lien immediately.

Time – we will figure out ways to maximize the facility as time goes by. I assure you I have a few more ideas.

Proposal – 50/50. I have no money. I have great credit. I have lots of ideas. I will find these properties and get them started. If you want to be hands on or off, I don't care. You may be telling yourself this is a great idea and I'll do it for myself for 100%, but I will not include you in the next idea. I also am making you aware unless we can pin this up for just us, I will also present this to other investors.

Personal – other investors may be alternatives for both of us, but I want to do this with you. Because we talked about TRUST.

Close-- I bring to you an income producing property with very little expense and maintenance. I also don't mind the fact that the property is potentially appreciating.

Miscellaneous ideas – coin-operated climate controlled devices – heat – air-conditioning – secured vending – snacks, drinks, ice cream, oil and other fluids commonly used – combination hands-free and hands on car wash – I don't mind squatters as long as they have the right attitude and do not try to reserve racks for their own customers – leasing is okay, but I would like to negotiate a purchase up front and possibly do a rent to own, with like a seven-year balloon owner financing – after all, our goal is to hold on to this income producing property until the demand is so great for the property, we must sell and take the profit. – www.my-tronic.de Is a website a friend told me would accomplish the money collecting machines. – forget Barney, how about video surveillance? Automatic rental paint booths – vending paint, tape, sandpaper etc. -- No loitering no exceptions. If you don't have money in the meter, you are not welcome – automated tire machine – alignment machine – put payment machine in a position where it can be fed in or out of the working stall, so when the doors come down and if you are still in, you have to pay to get out – after creation of our model auto hobby shop, we will sell franchises and put the model on the web to market and sell a whole turn key business constructed on your lot. Market retirees, don't just die, leave your heirs an income stream and a LEGACY. Have a Will package to sell where the retiree can decide to give complete control to the heir or make it forever be an income stream.

Retirees – allow this retiree to decide what LEGACY they can afford and what they feel is in the best interest of their heirs.

Have a clause if the property values become worth more than the income stream, then everyone in the bloodline over 18 years of age gets an equal vote of what to do with the IPA. Tie – No change.

More income property ideas – we need more ideas besides this one, to max out every opportunity for even the poorest to leave a LEGACY. The retiree can choose a location or leave the decision to the heirs or to the TRUST. If the family is known to disagree, maybe choose yourself or a TRUST.

LEGACY – I am selling LEGACY here, to everyone who wants to be remembered. We will have to give seminars at retirement homes and we can have salespeople do that. We can offer people rich or poor, a chance to leave a LEGACY without having a clue how to do it. Think about how many inheritances that are squandered. I will not let this idea down. This will be my LEGACY to mankind. Thank you Lord. We can buy existing businesses at fair market value. Leaving existing management and give the heirs the right to fire, only if production is not met. The heirs can run the business if they want to, but they are expected to meet the same expectations and can draw a reasonable salary. Stay out of court clause. If this deal does not make the heirs happy, then they can go against the retiree's wishes and with a majority bloodline vote, cash in.

I started to say screw all the partners, but I thought about what Jesus would do with this gift I've been given. SHARE.

The idea – sell a document to retirees that allows the inheritance to be used for what and how the retiree would like to invest in. If the dollar investment is too small for real estate, we will invest it into mutual funds. All the heirs can move around funds with a bloodline vote. Again if contested, a bloodline vote could result in cashing out losers. This is a hell of a gift to be given, to only turn your nose at it and want to squander your forefathers life's work.

LETTER TO:

MEL GIBSON

Dear Fellow Messenger,

I had to debate with myself before writing that, but I felt like if you knew where this was coming from, you would understand. I'm tired, broke to my standards and don't see any way out. I just let the people I love the most, down. In many ways, it is what brought me here to this hotel to write to you. After I let my loving parents down, I made it even worse by avoiding contact with them, like they were Bill Collectors. How sad. My guilt had overtaken my understanding of why I am truly here. Honor thy Mother and Father kept ringing through my head. All the years dealing with turmoil amongst my own family. I couldn't understand why we couldn't get along. I'll borrow that one from Rodney. We have been trapped following the wrong course. I couldn't see any other course, but I started to realize that it didn't matter how hard I worked, the situation was never getting better.

My dad kept over and over and over, do you have a BACKUP PLAN??? which made me want to avoid the call even more. I don't blame him. He was freaking out that all he had saved for on a meager source of wages was being blown by me, thinking I'm on the right course. My dad made the right decision, he cut me loose. A good friend of mine was on my mind driving back after a grueling week of being in the rat race and missing my children grow up. I called Brian because the last time I had talked to him, he sounded upbeat. I had decided for a career change and thought he may have some ideas. He gave me a book called Rich Dad Poor Dad and it hit me like a ton of lead. Friday, September 10, 2004 I was given a gift. This book was about me. I have two mentors that I dearly love. This is delicate and not meant to offend anyone. The gift I had been given, showed me that both of my mentors were right and wrong. I then was shown the right course, it has never been clearer. Friday night I tasted the book, but we had just come back from the football game with my son and five friends, my daughter and her friend. But I was still determined to taste this knowledge some more. After all, I have never let anyone with any degree of TRUST down. Until now and the person that I didn't want to let down the most, I did. I thought of all kinds of schemes on how I could get over on the credit companies, but that just went against my grain. I like being honorable and I like honorable people, but my naivety about other people pretending to be honorable got over on me. You can't tell what is in their soul, to take advantage of my heart. I try again and again to mentor people myself. I realized after I had been taken advantage of, that there are people that will set out to deliberately take advantage. I'm going to let this person in my life off the hook. Because we were both caught up in the rat race. Back to business. I started exploring my mind to find that backup plan my dad talked about. This new gift had been the catalyst. Before I could even get through the half way point, I got my sprinkle.

You see this was Sunday night after attending early service where Terry Ellis was preaching about guilt. And Man, do I have got the Lion's share. That morning I was there by myself and Jim Dillon asked to sit next to me. No one had ever asked to sit with me before. I have been going to church regularly, mostly by myself and it's as if there is something wrong with me. I admit that I did not get in line with the dress code. I don't know why, but I wanted to stand out. My seat was always available. I felt like the spotlight was on me. Being someone of many insecurities, this was a bold move. My wife fought me tooth and nail. She even used my dress as an excuse not to go to church with me. Just got a call from one of my mentors. By the time I was able to drive from Mobile to Atlanta, he was to shoot down my first good, get out of the rat race scheme. You see I have always had ideas. A lot like Michael Keaton in the movie Night Shift. A lot of my ideas have been just as crazy as "feed the tuna fish mayonnaise". I guess my track record of ideas and my stupid drinking escapades had blinded my entire family. The last to be blinded was my dad, who believed in me and I let him down. Because I did not know how to make money work for me. I had all my stupid ideas shot down so many times, all that was left for me was a job. I am the prodigal child. After all the ideas I had created failed, my family was not willing to believe in me any longer. But I was allowed to clear my debt with my dad and get a job, so I could be just like everyone else. $aving to wealth. My dad did it, I saw the struggle it took to acquire the wealth. I also saw my other mentor with plenty of material things and I was tempted by that, turning my back on the true way of achieving wealth like my dad had done. My dad could be wealthy if he would have not been afraid to fail. I have a strong sense of guilt on this topic. I was taught this negative reinforcement as a child. Even with all of my drinking shenanigans, I still possess a core sense of moral values. I guess that they were passed to me by my parents without me even knowing it. What a great gift. I try hard not to show my emotion, because that is what I have been taught. If you let them see weakness, they will surely strike you down. But things touch my heart, I cry and I am embarrassed. But when in fact it is this empathy that I have, that makes me want to help people. I didn't always have this trait. I was drinking and living for today. This is probably the reason I love my wife so much, the balance sheet of faults weighed heavily against me. But the balance of assets weighs heavy for me as well and I wanted nothing in return, but to see my family happy.

One Sunday a short time ago, Terry preached about Jesus giving three men talents, one man received 10, one man received five and one man received one or two. Jesus told them go make something with your lives that will glorify Me, You and Your Fellowman. Take these talents and return the amount that belongs to GOD. Jesus does a progress report. The man that got 10 talents turned it into 20, the man that got 5 turned it into 10 and the man that got one or two, buried it in the sand and quickly returned it to Jesus with a big grin thinking he had done the right thing. Jesus does not make mistakes, but a little more input on how to make money would have helped. Especially the ignorant that can't do it for themselves. But the point was, make money in this beautiful creation I have provided for you, give me my share and have empathy for your fellow man along the way. Jesus was angry with the one that did not invest and I bet this man felt even more guilt ridden than I for failing my Father. Terry illustrates this as a lesson on tithing. I have a different view.

Maybe about a month ago, GOD chose to have confusion in my Sunday school class. We were left without a teacher. By the grace of GOD, Terry was recruited to teach. I can't exactly remember what Scripture he wanted to talk about, but when he started by not apologizing for having material things, but justifying it. I don't think he has any guilt about the church providing him a nice lifestyle. It's the always thinking that a man of GOD should be poor, thus enabling him to connect with more people philosophy . That's bull. This man works hard for his money to spread the word that there is hope. For a lot of people all there is is hope. It is a powerful tool. Some people allow it to be all they do. They expect GOD to do it for them. No one has shown me a way I can take my one or two talents and create a LEGACY or Heirloom or an Income Producing Asset. Therefore I have become a bad disciple for GOD. The talent of teaching people how to be good disciples is not taught in schools. It is a gift from a mentor. Unfortunately not all mentors are passing along the right message. There are many reasons that not everyone can achieve wealth. That is why I feel GOD's word is here. He knows that not everyone is going to get it. The rat race begins. Some people don't get it because of ignorance. The ones that do get it, get wealthy and some have tried to give back by writing How-To books. But they fall on deaf ears because most people have mentors that will not let them take the risk and insist they bury their talents in the sand. Terry interpreted the Scripture as a lesson of stewardship, I did too, but I also saw it as GOD's grace and approval that you prosper. Now that you got it, what are you going to do with it.

The first good idea I had to bring me out of the rat race is inconsequential. It was a capitalistic idea and I expanded upon it until I added so many income producing assets, that I ran out of room on the property. I get now how people make money work for them. As I was gleaming about how I was personally going to get out of the rat race. All I could think of was who I could share this news with. My favorite pupil, my yes-man for all of my crazy ideas. No one wanted to listen to all my ideas, so I had Ralph listen to me while he was on the clock. We shared all kinds of brainstorms and I was trying to mentor, when I myself didn't have a clue. Dad mentored Ralph and I mentored Ralph. Ralph is a convicted felon (selling drugs) that paid his debt to society through jail time and became a honest hard-working citizen. This system works if there is Hope after corrective discipline. Typically he had a hard time finding work. He busted away from all the crabs (a bucket of crabs is an analogy about how you can almost get out of the bucket and a crab drags you back down). It's not society keeping you down, you got a case of the crabs (Family – Friends – Government - Mentors). Ralph now owns two homes. He rented one out under a Government Section 8 program and is guaranteed to receive the rent and since he bought the house next door, he can monitor the rental. We are working on refinancing the house he lives in and combine both mortgages into one. The rental income just about covers the total new mortgage, so Ralph almost lives rent free. Not bad for a guy a few years ago was selling drugs.

What I am trying to tell you is that on my mission to help myself, I couldn't help but to think of others. I'm sure this is not an original thought. Still working my capitalistic mind I started to think about the LEGACY and Birthrights. My next idea was to market my product, an Income Producing Asset. We will sell the idea to older people to use their life insurance to purchase an IPA and a LEGACY will be born, instead of a inevitably squandered lump sum of money. I don't know if this will be taxed or not. In most cases when the poor are given more than they feel they deserve, they spend it as fast as they can get their hands on it. They do not understand how to handle money and quickly get back to their state of financial comfort zone. Whatever that zone may be.

But what if instead of cash, the heirs were given a LEGACY. An Income Producing Asset. The LEGACY policy would be the same as a life insurance policy, only the heirs could not touch, nor could they squander the principal balance. The LEGACY policy buyer can decide how to split up their inheritance, not with cash, but with IPA's. Let's say my policy is for $1 million, I may elect to have the family receive $200,000 immediately and that leaves me $800,000 to decide how I want to invest that will reap my heirs the best dividends. The policy buyer may decide that leaving the investment decisions up to the heirs would cause undo turmoil and he may elect to hire the services of a professional financial planner. If the professional can yield 12% and pay the family 6% in income and the asset grows by 6%, the LEGACY checks become larger as time passes to accommodate future generations. The rule of 72's kicks in and a LEGACY is born.

The policy buyer may elect to put the other $400,000 into real estate, again allowing the heirs to participate in the decision of which assets are purchased, only if the policy buyer feels that they are financially competent or not. If not, a management company would purchase it for the policy buyer. If the LEGACY policy is for a mere $35,000 it will take longer, but it could possibly become financial freedom for the heirs or at least an income stream for their bloodline. This is a true Birthright LEGACY. This is a gift given to the heirs by their blood in hopes they may have a better life than their own.

This is when GOD came down on me like an anvil. While I was trying to figure out how to fix my problem. I wanted everyone to join in. First for the money – GOD says it's okay to make money, no guilt. Then I realized by trying to add more to my idea, GOD has shown me how even the poorest of the poor may be able to achieve at least a modest sum of passive income. I'm not an accountant, but I would think this would alleviate some undue stress on the Social Security system, putting money back into a capitalistic society and everybody is happy. In fact, I think the government ought to buy a policy for everyone in the country. I would like to see how this really cycles out. If you think I'm in it for the money, you're right. If you think I'm in it to help my fellow man, you are right again. But if you Mel Gibson, as a messenger of GOD yourself, can reach Christian and non-Christians alike. People might not be as afraid of dying if they know their work in this world is done. They can meet our GOD knowing, I left a LEGACY and I made sure it's forever. It won't be a $35,000 casino night memory for my heirs.

But the prodigal son would now be able to free myself from the guilt of failure and knowledge of success. And start living life the way the Lord intended us to live it. Stress-free, enjoy every phase of all life cycles and watch them flourish. I want you to help me share this vision. Help us to go to the next promised land of contentment. As the prodigal child, I would like to give back also. I have many more ideas in parables. GOD is making me think like he did in parables. I would like to share these with you and the world. I only got these ideas this weekend, so call me when I can finish what Paul Harvey would say, the rest of the story.

I'm sorry I just can't stop thinking about all I want to tell you. But I believe I'm being directed by GOD to help mankind. Not just my immediate family. Sure I plan to pass along a huge heirloom and LEGACY to my family. I think I've just found my LEGACY. I'm the messenger to change the thought pattern of society to buy LEGACY insurance, not life insurance. These are all going to be just my thoughts from now on. I would like to end this letter, but I can't. I think you should know my goal by now, so excuse my rambling ideas from here on out.

I have no idea why GOD chose me to wear my hot pink shirt to church, I do not know why he wanted me to stand out. I have my own personal reasons to what drove me to the church. But I will say it was two or three years before I hit bottom. It's amazing why it took me so long to realize I was on the wrong path, after now seeing the right one. Don't get me wrong, I'm still broke today. But the blessings you and I could share with the knowledge of a LEGACY policy are endless and that in and of itself is all the wealth that I need. I think I stand a pretty good chance on Judgment Day. I'm a sinner, I am forgiven and unloved even by the crabs in the bucket that have no idea they are crabs. These are the crabs that pinch the hardest, your family.

My son begged me not to go out of town, so I tried something different in my Dead end career job and I stayed home that week. By Wednesday night I realized if I didn't get out of town, I wouldn't get a paycheck that week. I could not afford to go just one whole week and learn how to be involved in my families life, because the bill collectors were breathing down my neck.

My daughter is 14, she is 5'10" a blonde knockout. She's smart, athletic why wouldn't the rest of the girls hate her. She suffers from low self-esteem and these crabs pinch pretty hard too. I'm trying to teach her, but I'm afraid I've been away from her too long and we can't reconnect. I think. I have one more idea. In the book that Brian gave me Rich Dad Poor Dad, the author has designed a game that allows anyone to get a grasp of how the financial world works. I hope by it being a game such as real life, it might attract her attention so that I can mentor to her. This is what every child needs and craves, to be loved and mentored in the ways of life and how our Father wants us to live it. They don't teach that in school and by the time most graduate, commencement for the most part is a celebration of jumping into the rat race. If you do climb out of the bucket, but most don't, be cognoscente of your purpose for GOD.

Be fruitful, multiply and nurture your children. Teach them ways to avoid stress, teach them ways to understand GOD. I don't believe in force feeding GOD, I believe in setting an example. If my children are mentored correctly, I think I have a good chance they will find GOD on their own. I don't want them to go the prodigal son route unless GOD has something else planned for them that I cannot see.

I went to a football thing at my son's school, it was new so that's why I call it a thing. I was presented this golden opportunity to hear coach Curtis and the Seniors speak. Bring a ball and let the players autograph your son's Ball. Coach Curtis said he didn't want to push the younger kids like my son into playing, because he was afraid it would cause them to get burned out on it. He said given the opportunity to be exposed to it was enough. If your child has any interest in it, he will find it, develop it and enjoy it on his own terms. I believe that is how you let children find GOD. I think if my children or anyone's children come to know GOD, it will be because I planted the seed, but it was their idea.

They are hooked. The more we can get people hooked on GOD, the better the world will be. But what about the money? How can I be happy, I don't have any money? I made a commitment to go to this football function the week and I had the revelation to make my job work right there at home. The next week was upon us before I knew it. I was preparing to go out of town to get my meager wages to pay bills and the government. After staying in town a week, I sure needed a paycheck. So I left with high hopes of accomplishing my financial task early and being able to go home and take my beautiful son to an event to enjoy.

I had a terrible week and I was afraid I was going to have to cancel on my son once again. GOD once again intervened in my life. I had purchased a car for a client and either from my own lack of responsibility or bad communication, it didn't matter the blame was to be put on me, after all I am a messenger. So instead of canceling on my son, I could kill two birds with one stone. I could make myself out to be a hero to both my client and my son. I planned my attack to maximize my earning potential for that week. I set up my job the next day so my friend could buy for me. I toiled with the idea of asking my friend Gene or my new buyer Gordon. I decided to ask my friend what I should do with the commissions with my new buyer or with one of my closest friends. The closest of friends told me to choose him, I will do it for you because you are my friend. This man would lay down his life for mine. I have no question. I've never been to war and don't want to go, but if I have to protect the very world I and my future generation want to enjoy, I would go to the ends of the earth.

Only if they are right with GOD about this decision would they want to do this, but everyone has a different thought process. I just hope I was around long enough on the weekends for my moral fiber to rub off on them. GOD > Country > Self, TRUST in GOD, help your fellow countrymen and you don't have to worry about the self. Sorry with rambling again. The football thing I ended up killing myself to get to, I showed up disgruntled that I had to be there and I worked so hard to do it. I forgot to get out of the rat race long enough to enjoy one of GOD's many gifts, children. I missed out on what could have been a great Kodak moment because my guilt of not being able to produce enough money, robbed me of that memory. How can I learn from that mistake? I asked myself, can I try not to make it happened again? You will only have so many opportunities.

Not everyone will be able to hear this message, but maybe with your help we can touch each and every one of them with a LEGACY of their own to pass down to all future generations of their bloodline. I think GOD is using me to get to you, so we can show everyone another direction. That direction is to never miss another moment with your kids, even if you are physically there. If money is what's keeping us from enjoying life. GOD says to me (NOT LITERALLY) share your knowledge with all and the ones that can hear, let them prosper. The ones that can't hear, we all must pitch in and educate them or we will just have to end up doing it for them anyway.

Government LEGACY policy. The Lord said the poor and ignorant will always be among us. So if we can't teach them to fish, we must provide an endless fish basket. But let's pull as many of the crabs out of the bucket as we can. In Sunday school, a great tenacious man and his supportive wife gave the lesson. I don't exactly remember what he was talking about, but

I do know he kept saying, "I can't wait to see Jesus". This is very profound to me. My mind wandered off the discussion now and I was wondering what his life must be like. Gene Hawkins? I had just started these booster shots of GOD three years ago. Gene was in the rat race and was handicapped while out trying to provide for his family. While I am new to GOD, I felt guilt that this man must know GOD. He must have a personal relationship that none of us could even fathom. I know he can't wait to see Jesus. I admire the fact that he has the tenacity to play the hand he was dealt and find peace that he has a gift to spread the word to other people. I think he is a messenger. I think like all of us would hope to be, his self-esteem is challenged and he is risen to the challenge. Never mind all the times I have been knocked down, only to get back up and try again. No one could ever imagine the will power it must take to meet the challenges of everyday life for this man. Yet he does it, I pray for him to continue his plight that GOD himself has put this man on.

Everyone we know and don't know, has their own issues. I remember bringing up my financial woes to my locksmith I've used for years. He says you think you got problems, let me tell you about mine. He one upped me that day, because it hurt my heart. Not that his wife had cancer, but the fact that I could not get past my own self-pity to offer a little more empathy at the opportune time. That man needed a hug, but I couldn't get out of the rat race long enough to realize that. I'm sorry, I will pray for him and his beautiful wife.

When I get the nerve to do something with this letter, it may or may not come to pass that I might be rewarded for sharing my knowledge. I could feel guilt for saying that, but I believe whatever you put in, you get back 10 fold. I don't know what wealth feels like. I would like to experience it, to see if I could get my creative juices going and find more ways I can help people get out of the rat race. I believe this is my mission. I was told in sales when you give the people what they want, you get what you want. I'm offering what they absolutely must have or our economy will feel strong ramifications. We can't pay all the baby boomers their Social Security benefits, it would break us. A bean counter might say this is not true, but why do we even need to find out. By making this one little adjustment. Give me a little more time to think and I might be able to come up with some ideas that would even expand on this one. Maybe everyone could start coming forward through you and reach the masses. Man are you up to that challenge. We better hire someone to screen all the mail and get to the ones with ideas that can make our way of life better.

I worked for Saturn, I like the philosophy. Let's allow everyone to put in their two cents and will vote on what would be the best thing for our country. I feel like most Americans, the only time I have a voice is at the voting machine. Which is bogus, because the media controls what people see and hear. Just one uninformed person swayed by advertising or tradition and will not take the time to get educated, will cancel out my vote. Give the people back the power. Use the government to protect it, develop it, for the people of America and quite possibly the world. Keep the ship going the right way and let our minds go where no man has gone before.

An open line of communication. That's interesting, maybe it's always been there, I'm just too ignorant to know it. I just now know that I have an open line of communication with GOD. I don't mean I can hear him actually, but I do feel him moving me. Terry gave a sermon on contentment. Enjoy life during the meantime and look forward to the extraordinary events. This is beautiful, let's add one thing. I am also working on my IPA's to provide my LEGACY to my children and my children's children. I spoke with another friend today while I was at the auto auction trying to effectively do my rat race job. It was difficult to stay focused on it, when all I wanted to do was put more ideas down on paper. My friend allowed me the time to share my vision. He tried his best to interrupt what I was trying to say, so as to add his two cents. A lot of the discussion was about cutting back expenses and living within my means. I have heard that sermon 'til I'm blue in the face, but somehow we got on the subject of healthcare. I'm enjoying overcoming objections, because the product that I am trying to sell is a concept that no rational person can tear down.

My product is now a very vivid vision, but there are always ways of maxing out a good idea or even a vision. I thought about all the people that don't have healthcare. Mainly because the premiums are high and in these economic times, insurance is one of those bills that probably will lapse or never gets purchased. Healthcare is a problem, so here's my vision. I can't really do much in the short run, but in the long run I think it will change everything. What I mean is, if these IPA's were set up properly, their yield would pay the premiums. I discussed earlier about the IPA providing a stream of income and growth at the same time. But if the IPA was earmarked by the policy buyer to pay for health care insurance premiums first and the remainder of the yield was split into reinvesting and a monthly inheritance check. The heirs gift would allow them to pay for their own healthcare insurance, reinvested growth and get a monthly check for living expenses. If we cannot get people on the bandwagon themselves, I believe we the people need to pay those premiums. We are handing out money left and right anyway. Why not make this investment so maybe by the time our great grandchildren come around, everyone will have healthcare.

It shouldn't be a quality standard of the type of health care you receive based on your income. If the premium is paid, its paid. I rarely have to pull money out of my pocket except for deductibles and co-pays and when I say healthcare, I mean prescription drugs as well. I don't know much about prescription drug costs, because I don't have anyone immediately close to me that has had a problem. I do know sometimes these great insurance plans are actually bogus. If I can get prescription drugs with insurance, they cost $100 this is supposedly charged to the insurance company and my percentage that I have to pay is 20%. I give the pharmacist 20 bucks. The next person behind me gets the same drug over the counter with no insurance for $18.50. I caught something about this on the Rush Limbaugh show. The numbers are arbitrary, but the concept is the same. It sounds like an old car dealer trick. If a customer comes back to the dealer and complains about transmission problems and the dealer tells them we will go 50-50 at our shop. We change the transmission that cost $850 and create a bill for $2000 and the customer pays $1000. I don't understand why people can't help other people. Because when you do, you're going to get paid.

I believe the motivation for buying life insurance for most people is to handle all of the burial expenses and to leave the heirs a gift. Wouldn't it be great if the salesman presented this option. Option 1: $100,000 cash to be dropped on my son at one time, he has had so many years that I have worried about him. I hope this money will straighten out his life. Option 2: LEGACY insurance $20,000 to my son in one lump sum. I hope this will help him with his credit card debt. But he never got the knack of managing money, so I would like the remainder invested into IPAs. $40,000 into the market and $40,000 in some kind of real estate that he can never sell unless the property becomes so valuable, that a wise investor would sell and reinvest the money for more opportunities. But don't give him any of the money. This is the great part. The person who is buying this policy would like for my son's health insurance premium and whatever else I deem necessary to sustain his life. Then whatever is left will be split 50-50. 50% reinvest 50% monthly paycheck.

The checks will start out small. But man watch out. This is the easiest decision I have ever made. If the heirs contest, use the bloodline vote. All blood relatives over the age of 18 have a vote to cash in or live with the dying wishes of someone that loves you enough to take the time and think of your future. Option one is a gift certificate. Once you get it, you spend it and you forget where it came from. The LEGACY checks can read whatever you want forever. I want mine to read “don't work for money, let money work for you”. And as those checks come in the mail, I hope my heirs discuss with their children what that means. And my LEGACY is born.

I just got off the phone with my wife. They are hunkering down to face hurricane Ivan, I am in Atlanta writing this letter. I can't afford to miss this week's meager paycheck, so I asked if they want to come up here for the worst day. Me coming home is really not an option. I don't want to live this way anymore and I did not see what my dad was asking me to do. Backup plan, backup plan. It made me sick to my stomach because I was being told you better figure it out quick, or we are going to lose the farm so the speak and I would lose all respect from my loving dad. I guess you might have called me that son that got the hundred thousand dollars in inheritance, because I can sure blow it trying to keep up that lifestyle. But when I started taking cash advances of future inheritance to the point of crippling my parents portfolio, my dad was right to stop me. (Author Notes: Does the U.S. Fiscal state mirror the same financial nightmare I am in? Who will be our Daddy? Mr. Federal Reserve? It's bad enough that the one talent man buried his talents in the sand, but now he is spending our future away).

That's when all my prayers were answered. GOD was in control now, I could not have come up with this vision all on my own. I'm just a car salesman with a lot of stupid ideas to make money. My wife just called and she had already heard from her parents, one of my mentors. I don't know what was discussed, but I have a pretty good idea. I didn't want to discuss this vision with my wife. Hold on another message came through, George Costanza wanted to be a talk show sportscaster. I don't know why in the series I missed that part. His mentor Jerry Seinfeld told him that sounded like a great idea. Then George says, how do those guys go about getting those jobs? Jerry says, that's where it gets a little tricky. Then Jerry assumes the role of a mentor and suggest George forget the whole thing and go back to the way things were and everybody will forget he went a little nutty. Jerry says, “hey you're entitled”. But now, welcome back to the real world. Many mentors have great words of wisdom and you should heed them, but subject them to critical analysis. Be careful who you listen to. I switched over to cassette tapes at this point because my fingers began to bleed. There are hours of tape I sent to Oprah Winfrey. I then concentrated on getting to Orlando to do my day job. Riding through the devastation Hurricane Ivan had left in its wake.

What a Nightmare!

LETTER TO:

PRESIDENT GEORGE W. BUSH
AND REPLY

Nathan J. Isbell
P.O. Box 592254
Orlando, FL 32859
Phone: 251 – 401 – 9039

Dear President George W. Bush

I think that I may have an answer to a lot of the dilemmas we all face together. It's called a LEGACY policy. All it is, is an adjustment for life insurance policies. Instead of just assigning the full amount of the policy to the beneficiaries, the policy purchaser would have a simple, easy-to-follow addendum. You can allocate a certain amount of cash to pay immediately to cover the cost involved for burial and anything else he deems necessary. The remainder would be invested into the market and managed by whoever he sees fit. 50% of the first fruits of the yield will be reinvested and the remainder to cover healthcare premiums and what is left be sent out in a monthly LEGACY check. If the yield after the 50% reinvest will not cover the health insurance premiums, then we the people must subsidize the rest. We are covering healthcare cost anyway. If the heir has health insurance through a job, then reinvest 50% and send out a LEGACY check for the other 50%. As time goes on and the rule of 72's kicks in, these checks can get very sizable. Maybe even one day alleviating the taxpayers the burden of supporting all types of welfare plans. We all are concerned as the baby boomers reach retirement age, that there will not be enough Social Security money to pay out unless we go back to the taxpaying citizen for more money. I hope that my great-grandchildren are not faced with that dilemma. But with LEGACY policies in place we should find ourselves not having to subsidize the money near as much and maybe one day not at all. I understand the volatility of the market. There are many ups and downs, but that is where the beauty of dollar cost averaging comes into play. The people that don't have life insurance at all should be forced to have it, even if the taxpayer buys it for them, maybe a $10,000 policy. If the person is employed, have the employer pay it and give him a tax credit. If the person has no job, then the taxpayer will pick up the tab. It's an investment for the future. I believe it is better to get this, something similar or better started. Rather than have to hand out checks for the rest of that person's life.

By having all of these LEGACY policies invested into the market, I believe that this will give the United States a new foundation, because this money is earmarked never to be drawn out or liens put against it. Not even the government can get their hands on it. Ex: Social Security. I am sure that there are plenty of ways the program can be implemented, but I would prefer to go out to the people of the United States. To the free enterprising Capitalistic marketplace, thus not becoming bogged down with the typical Government bureaucracy. The welfare portion of the plan will probably have to be administered by the government. It's as simple as getting on TV and explaining the program and having people convert their existing policies to a LEGACY policy. The proper spokesman should be carefully determined. Maybe Mel Gibson, he has already captivated audiences worldwide with his movie Passion of the Christ, but already the movie has found its way to Blockbuster and the people have slipped into their normal routine.

When I tried to do this with my investment broker, I was told that I would have to hire an attorney to draw up this document and it would cost approximately $500 to do so. This would be enough to stop most people from setting up something that would pay their bloodline forever. I read an advertisement from Prudential that they had something like this, but I doubt that it's as intense or would encompass all US citizens.

Being a part of the tail end of the baby boomer generation, born in 1962. I would like to be a part of a generation that reinstated birthrights and Legacies for all future generations, rather than a generation best known for sucking the economy dry and left future generations the bill. I believe future generations would prefer getting a monthly LEGACY check, rather than a monthly tax bill. Your staff has much more financial intelligence than I. I just wanted to throw out the idea and let the creative mind of the human being expand upon it and find a winning solution.

May GOD bless America and the World,

Nathan J. Isbell
Common Taxpayer

CC: Robert Kiyosaki
Oprah Winfrey
Rush Limbaugh
Bill O'Reilly
Sean Hannity

LOST BOOKS OF:

THE PROPHET NATHAN

Dear Reader:

Thank you so much for sharing your ideas with us. Unfortunately, due to the sheer volume of material we have at hand, we are unable to incorporate your concept. We wish you much success in placing your idea elsewhere, and thank you for your interest in *O, The Oprah Magazine*.

Sincerely,

The Editors

1700 BROADWAY | 38TH FLOOR | NEW YORK | NY 10019 | T 212·903·5187 | F 212·977·1947

LETTER TO:

PASTOR TERRY ELLIS

SPRINGHILL BAPTIST CHURCH
MOBILE, ALABAMA
AND REPLY

Letter to Pastor Terry Ellis
written at an auto auction.

Dear Terry,

I now understand why you and others would think that I had lost my mind. I was in the middle of my own shock and revelation phase. I believe this happens to everyone when they finally find GOD. I hope this letter to the President clears up any misunderstanding about where I was trying to go with my ideas. I have found that people are very attracted to the shock and awe method. It worked for Howard Stern, Janet Jackson and the War in Iraq. Why can't it work for GOD? Our society has become very callused and unfeeling for others. Always looking out for our own first and only after, if any empathy is left, look out for others. I believe in the Scripture about us being judged by how we help our fellow man while we go through this trial and error period we call life. I believe we are all still partying at the bottom of Mount Sinai. We still haven't reached the promised land.

I remember a time in Sunday school win Rich something announced he had been given the opportunity to examine the church records and found how poorly our own class was tithing. I witness embarrassment, guilt and even outrage. One member, to remain nameless, I believe he spent many hours praying for forgiveness for his own comments. He lashed out and said "how about I start billing the church for the man hours my wife and I contribute and use that as our tithe". Everyone had their own emotions that day, but they probably went unshared. I myself, took it as a wake up call from GOD and started trying to give more. My own financial situation would not allow me to tithe and I felt guilty and asked GOD for forgiveness.

We have witnessed extraordinary events even in our own church. I thought about what may have been going through

Donnie Mayes mind when he executed his wife Kay. Could he have been doing all in his power to provide a nice house, car and private schools for his family? Could he have been driven by a strong-willed wife that could not fathom the thought of having to scale back financially? Is that why he embezzled money from his employer, because his present salary would not support that lifestyle? Could that be what caused him to go to the edge and not have any more solutions or options? I can relate. Fortunately for me, my moral fiber and tenacity was stronger than his.

I have put many thoughts on tape and I hope it will become a book. I will call it "Shock GOD". I would try to tell you what is in it, but there are too many subjects to even write down, I tried. I will just tell you that anything you can think of controversial, is in it. There are over 30 hours of tape about how I believe Jesus would have wanted us to handle it. I have also started a new book "Financial Bible" from my samplings of the book Rich Kid Smart Kid by Robert Kiyosaki. He covers the importance of teaching our children how to survive in the real world after graduation. I add my own spiritual comments to his, thus creating a Financial Bible. I believe all churches should start up this class, because it is not being taught in schools and most parents do not have the financial IQ to share it with their children. Even if they wanted to. I want to thank you for being my friend and Pastor. Please pray for me, that I find my way through the many challenges that I must face. But I have chosen GOD's path and even if this book never comes to pass with GOD's grace, I will have fulfilled my mission. I am a sinner, but with GOD's grace I am forgiven.

May GOD bless us all, Everyone

Nathan J. Isbell
Common Believer

P.S.

here's another one of my crazy ideas. If the book flies, I plan to keep 10% for myself 10% for (1st Wife) 10% for Lauren 10% for Austin and 10% for my Mom and Dad. The other 50% to be invested into a LEGACY account to build a facility designed to help people with all types of health and emotional problems for free .

October 3, 2004

Nathan,

I'm glad you called today. It was good to hear from you and to know that you are well. I hope everything works out soon for you to make the life in Orlando that you envision. I am also glad to hear of your continued commitment to taking care of Karen and the children under what are difficult circumstances for all of you.

I have enclosed the material you brought to me before you left town. As I told you, I am not a salesman and am ill-equipped to help you implement your ideas. The best I can offer is to be a friend and pastor, and I pledge to offer you continued support in both those roles.

The changes you are facing and have brought about are unsettling to those around you. They may not have reacted the way you would want. They may feel the same way about you. I'm sure you understand that. These situations are difficult and seldom play to our strengths. The most important advice I can give you, if you asked, is to make sure you give as much grace as you can. God has a way of working when His people are committed to grace.

Take care Nathan. I pray God's blessing on you. Let me know if I can help you.

Your friend and pastor,

Terry Ellis

REPLY FROM:

PASTOR DAVID LOVELESS

DISCOVERY CHURCH
ORLANDO, FLORIDA

DAVID LOVELESS
SENIOR PASTOR

Discovery Church
4400 S. Orange Avenue
Orlando, Florida 32806
407.855.3140

November 17, 2004

Dear Nathan,

Thanks for allowing me to read over the document you sent to the president and other influential leaders.

I am glad you want to be on the solution side of building a legacy for future generations. I commend you for your heart and passion.

Sincerely,

Discovery Church is a growing community dedicated to raising up fully devoted followers of Jesus Christ, who are making an eternal difference with their lives.

LETTER TO:

BILL HOLMES
HOLMES MOTORS INC.

For Bill Holmes Eyes Only

To: Bill Holmes
From: Nathan J. Isbell
Re: Tough decisions made by tomorrow's leaders

Bill,

I could tell in our conversations this week that an overwhelming amount of grief loomed in your heart. One can only imagine what could be going on in your mind, faced with all of the life altering decisions that you and only you can make. After we spoke Thursday night, I felt compelled to enlighten you as to the reason for my and many others demise in business. Why you are a pioneer in business, while myself and so many others fail. Do you remember the movie "You've Got Mail"? Tom Hanks repeats over and over again to Meg Ryan that it's not personal, it's business. You could actually tell that it was hurting him, but he knew what had to be done and had been schooled in the proper way to run a free capitalizing enterprise. Unfortunately, there are always some that get hurt in the process and they have to make adjustments in their own lives. Many times these same people end up finding themselves in the process and go on to make much more out of their lives. Careers they would have never achieved as long as they had their safety net to fall back on.

This scenario also exemplifies our business relationship. I understand that the job of buying cars at a fair market price is crucial to the long-term existence of Holmes Motors. I am also very aware that if I'm not able to achieve this task, someone will have to. As I write this to you, I realize I may be writing my own epitaph, but the facts only speak for themselves. You are the one that is ultimately responsible for the well-being of the company and its continued success or its failure. If I had only had the ability to position myself to make those tough decisions that you have made and have to make daily, in my own business and personal life, there would be no telling where Nathan's Auto Sales and Nathan Isbell would be today. I can only think back and say, what if I had done this. I hope I have learned from my mistakes. Being a person with a kind heart has many advantages, but can have many detriments as well.

I know you well enough now to know you didn't come into this decision process blind. When you elect to employ friends and relatives, you also elect to take on the inevitable task of discipline and work termination. Now is one of those times and the hardest question you have to ask yourself is, are these changes in the best interest of Holmes Motors? If they are – just do it and stick to your guns, knowing that you have spent many painstaking days making your decisions that could directly influence the stability of your own family sphere. I don't envy you of your task, but you're the one that took on the task of being the leader and there are a great many families that are glad you did and only pray for your continued success. Not everyone has a special gift to lead or the tenacity to get beat down day after day, only to get back up and try again. This is something to be very proud of and not ever lose. If you will remember, I truthfully told you and Shirley about resembling the Fezziwig's (Scrooge). The Fezziwig's were a couple that always were caring and loving amongst their employees. They tried to always create an environment that anyone would want to work in. I believe you and Shirley both possess the rarest characteristics that can only be found in Fortune 500 companies.

The night you showed me around your town was very illuminating. From the stories of how you started your enterprise and career selling candy at the school, paper route, lawn care business, building your first home with your bare hands and ultimately amassing your own small empire. I don't believe any of this could have been accomplished had it not been for your moral turpitude and your undying compassion for your fellow man. One man cannot achieve all of this alone, it takes the support and infrastructure of a team. Teams only succeed when there is a strong leader they like and respect. One that makes tough decisions about carefully weighing out the options. I believe you have always conducted your life in such a manner, always putting the needs of the many ahead of your own. You don't ask anyone to do anything that you yourself would not do, which is very very rare in your position and you should expect no less from your subordinates. In fact, I have preached to you about delegating a little more, but you are stubborn and only time will educate you in that fashion. Bill, with my own 17 years in the automotive industry, on occasion there is a special person that comes along and touches other's lives. Even if our future does not permit my continued employment, I will always appreciate your wealth of knowledge that you have the bestowed upon me.

If I can ever be of assistance to you regardless of my own personal and business endeavors, I hope you know that I will always be there for you.

Mi Casa, Su Casa
Your Real Friend,
Nathan J. Isbell

LETTERS TO:

JERRY PILGRIM ESQ.

To: Jerry Pilgrim Esquire
From: Nathan J. Isbell
Re: Reasons leading to divorce

On or about May 2002, (1st Wife) requested a new dining room set for her birthday. Already struggling with the bills, I tried to explain that we were just not in any kind of financial situation to buy it. She explained that it was her 40th birthday and she felt that she deserved it. So to keep the peace in the household, I made the purchase. Shortly after this purchase she became discontent about our living room furniture, so on or about May 2003 I purchased a new leather sofa and several other assorted items. Sometime on or about September 2003 the bad news of her father becoming ill with cancer came out. This came as very bad news for obvious reasons and also he had become my true source of income and he had even told me that I would have to find a new way to replace the inevitable decline in my income.

I tried many different ways to replace the income and actually created more losses than gains. As long as he was at the dealership buying the cars direct from Nathan's Auto Sales, I managed to get by and pay the bills with no extra and quite possibly at a slow loss. On or about October 2003 (1st Wife) expressed extreme discontent about the house we were living in and wanted to move to the Spring Hill area, so that she could be close to all the activities that she and the children were involved in. We have been trying to sell the house for quite some time at a price that would cover the entire indebtedness and I knew that it would never happen. So during the month of October 2003 (1st Wife)'s father had said that he would help with the inequity in our existing house with a personal contribution of $31,000. I again explained to (1st Wife) that we were in no condition financially to make this move, but I agreed to reduce the price and the house sold quickly. After the $31,000 was used for the inequity, my parents contributed $10,000 to help with a 5% down payment needed on the new house. The payments were to increase from a first and second mortgage totaling approximately $1500 to a new first of $2023, but after one year we could get it reduced by dropping the PMI. The house we purchased has enough equity to do this and I knew it.

Between me and my parents, we reconditioned the house without any help from (1st Wife). I would leave on Mondays to go to Orlando, stop in to help my in-laws on Thursday nights and get home on Friday. On the weekends I would work on the house, then start the process all over again. Sometime in 2004 after working on the house, I was lying in bed with (1st Wife) and telling her how much I loved her and how beautiful she is and she looked me straight in the face and asked me what I was going to buy her. On or about May 2004 (1st Wife)'s father's health was fading and had to be admitted to the hospital. She made only one trip to see and help her father, stayed one day and then took off to the beach to stay at her family's condo. During the same time frame, I had spent several nights at the hospital assisting her mother, so she could go home for rest. The last time I stayed with (father in law), (Mother in law) came in the next morning and offered to compensate me. My emotions were running high at the time with lack of sleep and it caught me off guard and I broke into tears. I wasn't there for compensation, I was there to help my family. I arrived home to (1st Wife) and she advised me that the next time her mother offers me money, that I was to take it and put it in a envelope and bring it to her.

On or about June 2004 I had been put on a buyers fee with (City) Honda and my income was severely decreased. I went to (1st Wife) to plead with her that I needed her help financially and asked her to get a job. I told her that if she didn't try to help, we were possibly headed for bankruptcy. Her response was that I may go down, but she would land on her feet. She also informed me that her father was paying for the children's education at UMS to the tune of $1500 a month and that is what both she and her father considered as her financial contribution to the well-being of the family and the idea of her getting a job was just not going to happen. This was also confirmed by her father. I tried to keep up with the bills, but it was getting worse and worse.

On or about August 2004 (1st Wife) told me that her parents had told her that she would not receive any type of inheritance, because they felt like I would take the money and pay off my parents the debt we owed them. I believe this gave her an incentive to get rid of me. When Hurricane Ivan came through I knew that my parents were going to lose their home and I was in no condition to keep up the mortgage payments for the loan they had taken out to help us.

On the way to Atlanta to sell cars, I had begun exhausting my brain to come up with ideas to make money and then ultimately turned to GOD for help. This is what started the whole idea that I had lost my mind and made (1st Wife) not want me to return to the household. I left the household because she said that she was afraid of me, so I went to Orlando to perform my job. She felt like I had abandoned them, filed for divorce and took out a restraining order. I depleted all the funds left over from a car deal that I was out of TRUST with my dad and had to file bankruptcy. I didn't realize that by filing bankruptcy that I would ultimately lose my ability to attend the auto auctions, so I lost my job of buying cars for the one account that I had left. I decided to relocate back to Mobile and try a new career in real estate.

Date: 01/16/2005
To: J. Jerry Pilgrim Esquire
From: Nathan J. Isbell
Re: Request for reasons leading to divorce

The Monday prior to Hurricane Ivan's arrival, I had to make a decision whether to go to Atlanta to represent my five cars that I had sent there to sell or stay home. The transportation cost was $500 and they were due to be paid off to my floor plan company. I sought approval from my wife and advice from my father-in-law. Both agreed that I needed to go and represent them. We did not know for sure where the hurricane would land at this point. I offered to go to Ft. Walton to borrow my in-laws generator in the event we lost power here and both parties said no.

As I drove to Atlanta I started to realize this hurricane could wipe out my parents home. This home was to be sold at the end of the month and pay off the debt I owe to my parents. I knew they couldn't afford the payment and based on my present financial situation, I could not afford it either. So as I drive to Atlanta I started exhausting my brain by coming up with ideas that could produce income. My first idea was a U-Fix-It shop. An idea conceived using the same principles as the coin operated car washes only with hydraulic lifts. This idea started me thinking towards an asset that produces income without having any labor costs. I started to think it may be able to be designed and marketed on the web. The concept of an income producing asset without labor made me think of another idea I had years earlier, altering the way life insurance policies were being sold. Refer to my letter to the President for the whole finished idea. When I tried to come up with how I would get my idea presented is where the problems all began. Trying to contact a celebrity was maybe a little over the top and hard for anyone to fathom, but I was in a desperate situation and grasping for straws.

By the time I reached Atlanta my father-in-law had already shot down the idea of the you fix it shop. So I tried to explain my concept of the LEGACY account to him and my wife. All they could lock onto was the way I wanted to get it presented via celebrities. They immediately took the response that I had lost my mind and needed psychiatric help.

As I sat in my empty hotel room I watched the weather forecast showing the most massive hurricane to hit the coast in years. I started to fear for my family's safety and begged (1st Wife) to drive to Atlanta. She refused and I may have gotten a little verbally forceful. She claimed the vehicle she had would not make it, but I had driven it extensively and found it to be quite roadworthy. When I accepted the fact that they were not coming, I suggested she walk across the street to check out the church facilities to find out what type of accommodations were provided and put together a package that may make their stay there a little more comfortable in the event they had to evacuate our home. She refused to do even this. During this time she and my in-laws had made up their minds that I was completely insane and needed help immediately. They phoned my parents and encouraged them to come to Atlanta and get me. My parents called me and after a lengthy conversation found me to be stressed, but in control of my mental facilities. After the hurricane had come and gone, I made sure everyone was safe and went to Birmingham to stay with my parents at my aunts house. We proceeded to complete my mental examination by me explaining what all was going through my mind. I had turned to GOD through prayer and begged for everyone's safety. This too prompted even more concerns by my wife and in-laws, that I was insane. I find it very interesting when you turn to GOD for help, your supposed loved ones really start to question your sanity.

The next day was Saturday and my dad and I proceeded to go home. They told me that my wife did not want me to come home, that she feared for her safety with me. Although I had never in the 23 years of being a part of her life, never showed signs of physical violence. My dad was to continue to Navarre Florida to find out if he had a home or not. His cell phone was not working properly, so I gave him mine. He is a full-blown diabetic and has little feeling in his feet and we were all concerned with him walking through the rubble injuring himself and not knowing it. His needs for a cell phone took precedence over mine.

When I arrived home I hugged my children and went upstairs to see (1st Wife). I put my arms around her and she said "what makes you think you can go off the deep end and just come back home?" She asked if I had arranged an appointment with a psychiatrist and I told her that I thought she was to make these arrangements and if it would make her feel more comfortable, I would gladly go. She said it was not her responsibility. She then asked me what page I was on. I asked her what page she wanted me to be on. I can't remember how this came up, but I explained that I did not have any extramarital activities going on, nor have I ever. She just shrugged her shoulders and said she didn't care about that. I then asked her if she was afraid of me, she answered yes. I could only see that our conversation was headed to a fight and did not want to be in any compromising situation by staying there. So I went downstairs and grabbed my luggage I came in with. My daughter asked me where I was going. So I lied and told her that I was going to check out my cars at the lot. I left the house and went to my minister's house to drop off my ideas I had been working on, hoping he would see that I was okay and understand that all I was doing what was coming up with ideas to better my financial situation. I soon learned that confiding in your minister doesn't necessarily mean confidentiality. He ended up turning everything I confided in him, over to my wife. This has certainly disillusioned me with organized religion, but not with my personal relationship with GOD.

I felt pretty confident my parents house had been destroyed and I would somehow have to make the mortgage payment. I didn't have a clue where to go, but as I drove down the interstate it dawned on me to try and sell my ideas to one of my employers. He was a secondary source of income, but since has become my only source. I met him and his wife, had dinner and discussed the you fix it shop. He liked the idea and plans to help finance and create it. We have done some research on military bases and found it to be a very sound business idea. They have something similar, but it is not coin-operated. Unfortunately, the idea would have to be put on hold because his resources are being dedicated to building a new dealership in Texas. They put me up at the hotel and invited me to their home Sunday to watch football.

On Sunday morning I decided I had better make my way to Orlando so I could go to work and earn some income. I knew the interstates would be in turmoil, so I left early. Having no phone I could not be contacted, nor could I contact anyone. It took all day for me to get to Lake City Florida where I stayed the night. I contacted my minister to let him know I was okay and to have him notify my family of such. He had not read my material in its entirety and felt like I was trying to get him to invest into something.

On Monday I continued to Orlando where they were bracing themselves for yet another hurricane. So the Auto Auctions were closed and all I could do was to hunker down and ride out Hurricane Jeanne myself. At this point in time, I started trying to contact my parents via my aunt. They were all frantic because two days had passed without hearing from me. They made arrangements to send my cell phone and once again, I could be reached.

When I spoke to my in-laws they explained (1st Wife) was done and wanted a divorce. I later found that she had filed for a restraining order as well. I knew the marriage was over and resolved to the fact I would just have to deal with it and figure out what direction to take my life as I had promised my parents. I would continue to keep my job and did not miss an opportunity to keep an income. But because of losing my father in law as an account and losing (City) Honda because they could not contact me during my cell phone dilemma, my income had been reduced to just one account. I had a little money left over in my account and used it to send to (1st Wife) during the following months. This money was not mine, but belonged to my dad from the vehicle I had floor planned with him and not paid back. At this point I think I should address the money. The Monday that I continued to Orlando, I drew all but $5000 out of my account. I did this because it wasn't my money and if (1st Wife) got it out first, I would have no control over the situation. I left $5000 to handle the household expenses. I also knew that (City) Honda still owed me $1800 and I figured this would be enough to handle all the bills.

I did not realize during my time of high anxiety that I had inadvertently forgot to deposit a check for payment of a vehicle for $6000. That is why checks started to bounce. I was very disoriented as to why I was bouncing checks, I felt like I had left $5000. (1st Wife) got drafts from my place of work and tried to deposit them. She claims she was doing me a favor. I shudder at the thought if the bank had been willing to cash them. I had planned for my floor plan companies to handle the transactions directly, but it is their policy to send drafts. While all the dust was settling there was still the question of approximately $5500 that I was waiting for the bank to clear. I planned to use that money to pay the bills after finding out the mix up with accounting. The bank had told me a date it would clear, but before that date came (1st Wife) had been checking daily with the bank and withdrew the funds. I confronted her with it to make sure she was the one that had gotten it. She claims she creatively acquired it. Which was fine, I had planned to give it to her anyway, why else would I have left the $5000 in there.

The money I drew out on Monday, I deposited into an investment account here in Orlando. I wasn't sure what to do with it. I should have just deposited it into my father's account, but it did ultimately subsidize the almost $4000 per month that I sent to (1st Wife) through December. After attorneys fees, psychological evaluations, monthly expenses and the auctions closing the holidays, I have depleted my account and can no longer send the amount I have been sending. During these few months that I have been isolated from my children due to the restraining order, (1st Wife) only allowed me one phone call per week to my son. I took the time to reinvent myself and hopefully find a career that could replace the lost income.

I have successfully completed a 63 hour real estate course, 24-hour mortgage broker course and a 40 hour home inspection course. I also passed the Florida real estate exam a task that only 33% of the applicants pass at all. I passed on the first attempt. I hope this shadows the results of my psychiatric evaluation stating I am unorganized and lack focus. I believe in my brief meeting with Dr. Davis he drew some erroneous conclusions based on me having a failed business. I have done all in my power to keep our family in a lifestyle that was expected, without any signs of support or appreciation. I could give you many examples, but don't find it necessary to demean (1st Wife). If my income should increase I will gladly increase my family contributions, but I ask the courts not to subject me to an amount that I cannot possibly afford at present. I believe (1st Wife) is a fine mother and will do a great job in raising our children despite her materialistic ideology. All I ask is to see the children based on the Alabama out-of-state visitation privileges and an equitable division of our existing assets.

March 27, 2005

To: Jerry Pilgrim Esquire
From: Nathan J. Isbell
Re: Parent's conference with Molly Sullivan

Dear Jerry,

My parents met with Molly Sullivan on Friday, March 25, 2005 and we discussed in length how the interview went. They told me that there were several circumstances that seem to be on the forefront of not allowing any visitation on my part. I would like to address these so that there is no misunderstanding of exactly what my intentions and thoughts are.

Accusation one – in my confidential letter to my minister, I wrote about how I could understand how Mr. Mayes could kill his wife. The paragraph is written exactly this way – we have witnessed extraordinary events even in our own church. I thought about what may have been going through Donnie's mind when he executed his wife Kay. Could he have been doing all in his power to provide a nice house, car and private schools for his family? Could he have been driven by a strong-willed wife that could not fathom the thought of having to scale back financially? Is that why he embezzled money from his employer because his present salary would not support that lifestyle? Could the fear of jail cause him to go to the edge and not have any more solutions? I can relate. Fortunately for me, my moral fiber and tenacity was stronger than his.

Rebuttal – somehow being able to relate and empathize to someone else's situation, because of the circumstances following so closely to my own, makes me guilty of plotting out the same outcome. I did not know Donnie or Kay at all. I have no idea what their circumstances were. I can only assume what could have been going on in his mind. This should in no way implicate my intentions of carrying out such a heinous act. I do however, understand how in today's social environment and media coverage, even writing such can be misconstrued. I was merely pointing out that I had been pushed to the edge by trying to maintain a lifestyle that was far above our financial means and with no support from my spouse, work related or even a sense of appreciation for my efforts. When things got bad financially, my request that (1st Wife) go to work to help out were shot down by both her and her father. (1st Wife) and her father considered his financial contributions of school support was in fact an $18,000 per year income for (1st Wife) and therefore she didn't have to work. So once again the entire financial burden rests upon my shoulders and I was completely exhausted through my efforts. Even pushed the lengths that I was, I would never even consider the idea of harming (1st Wife) or the children. In the 19 years of marriage and 24 total years of knowing her, I have never harmed her or the children.

Accusation two – (1st Wife) claims I threatened to push her down the stairs.

Rebuttal – this allegation comes from a telephone conversation I believe occurred sometime in October 2004. I was in South Florida at the time of the call, I hope she has this on tape because it would clear me of any wrongdoing. We were discussing the events of my departure and she kept claiming that I had abandoned her and the children. My response to her was that I had not abandoned them, but merely was trying to protect myself. She had already told me to my face and all significant others that she was in fear for her safety in my presence. I attempted to explain that by me being in her presence and if something were to happen to her no fault of mine, like falling down the stairs, I would be prime suspect number one. In light of all the media coverage concerning Scott and Lacy Peterson, I didn't think it was in my best interest to stay in the household, but all she wanted to hear was that I was going to push her down the stairs. If I had any intentions of harming her in anyway, I would've stayed in the household, not vacated the premises.

Accusation three – Dr. Davis certifies me to be Bi-Polar - manic – lack focus – unorganized – not able to manage money – sleep deprivation – and having grandiose ideas and in light of these allegations, I am not to see the children unsupervised until further psychological examinations can be conducted.

Rebuttal – I am still to this day not exactly clear on how Dr. Davis arrived at these conclusions. I called him to ask how he arrived at these conclusions. Was it something in the test questions, my motor skills, my problem-solving skills or my mannerisms? What was it exactly that would make you draw these conclusions? His reply to me was this "do you know how you told me, that at an auto auction you could walk around a car and be able to determine its value from your knowledge? It's kind of the same with my evaluation". Basically, he had informed me that I know my business and he knows his – not to be questioned. This type of answer is very convenient when you have no justification. I can certainly justify my valuation of a car. So delving a little further into his evaluation may have served helpful in my own demeanor. He may claim that I lack focus, but all of the courses that I have been taking in the last six months such as real estate, mortgage broker, home inspector and my 45 hour continuing education for real estate were passed with high marks and on the first attempt. It is possible that I am unclear on what lack focus truly means. Being organized is a trait that I was reprimanded for in my very first job and I have gone to great lengths to never allow this to happen again. I still have some pitfalls, but I believe my organizational skills to be quite good and better than most. Not being able to manage money is a trait that many of us struggle with. The claims that I hear are that the majority of US citizens are one months wages away from bankruptcy. The one comment he made to me about me telling him that I would go days without sleep is erroneous and I told him that I did not make that claim, for I have never been 24 hours without sleep before in my life. But my favorite allegations were the ones about having grandiose ideas. How could he know they were grandiose, every attempt to tell him the idea was cut short by his hand signaling me to stop and his statement of "its way over my level of comprehension". I can only conclude that his conclusions were derived from the fact of me having a failed business and I had angered him trying to quiz him for more information. His remedy of further evaluations to be conducted are understandable. If you have one party in a relationship making claims of emotional instability, why would anyone stick his neck out and give a clean bill of health after only a one-day evaluation. Even though this will cause more undue financial hardship, I am prepared to do whatever it takes to see my children unsupervised.

Accusation four – My parents are not attentive enough to allow them to be the supervisory liaison.

Rebuttal – it is true that Austin fell into water less than waist deep from my parents pier. He was eight years old at the time and a very active child. He is also old enough to conduct himself without the constant supervision of an adult. Children do have mishaps at this age and to expect that nothing is to ever to go wrong while a child explores the wonders of this world, would be naive. A one year old on the other hand, must have constant supervision. My daughter, while in the care of her mother was able to crawl to some cabinets and get a battery. She was unsupervised long enough to chew through the casing and acid burned her lips and mouth. She was rushed to Providence Hospital and treated and fortunately she did not suffer any lifelong scars from the event. But never did anyone question (1st Wife)'s attentiveness to the well-being of our child.

(1st Wife) has driven a wedge between my parents relationship with me and the children for many years. I have never been able to figure out why she wishes to alienate them, when all they have ever wanted to do was to help us and be of support. I can only surmise that she had grown up in an environment where her mother had in fact alienated her father's mother. Maybe there was justification in her case, but I never got to know her grandmother to draw my own conclusions. But by doing all of this alienation, it robbed my parents the gift of being grandparents to its fullest extent and kept me on pins and needles trying to keep the peace amongst the entire family. My parents are very attentive and loving and should not have to endure (1st Wife)'s mouth any longer.

As far as attentiveness goes, you should evaluate the fact that my son has now been put on some type of drug to calm him down in school. (1st Wife) wanted to do this years ago and I would not allow it. Three months after our separation and now Austin is on medication. The countless hours (1st Wife) spends on the phone conducting gossip sessions with her friends, may be time better spent with Austin and his school work. I know for a fact every time additional time is spent with him and his homework, he always received a much higher grade. He is not like Lauren, who has the ability to pick up on things on her own. He requires special attention which my parents in their limited number of visitations have always bestowed upon him.

My own accusation – (1st Wife) told me to my face that her parents told her that she would not be able to receive any financial inheritance in fear of me using the money to repay the debt to my parents. During the deposition, Grady asked a series of questions like – was Nathan a good husband? Yes. Was Nathan a good father? Yes. Was Nathan a good provider? Yes. You've been married for 19 years? Yes. So with all this considered, why wouldn't you go to Atlanta to check on your husband who you say was exhibiting, what you refer to as a radical behavior? I was afraid he would hurt the children. Couldn't you have left them in someone else's care? Yes, but I was afraid he would hurt me. Has he ever in the 19 years of marriage harmed you or the children in anyway? No. So 17 days after a man you say was a good husband, good father, good provider and only exhibiting radical behavior is why you elected to file for divorce and petition for a restraining order? Yes. Nathan tells me that you told him, that your parents couldn't leave you any inheritance due to him using the money to pay off his parents with it, is this true? I don't recall. – I believe this adds credibility that my statements are true. She wanted out of the relationship fast, due to her father's increasingly failing health, so that she could in fact reap some of the benefits of the inheritance. He did in fact pass on February 14, 2005 and I was never made aware of this. I found out through a third party and was very distressed that I was not allowed to pay my last respects to a man that I had respected and loved the last 24 years. Because of time, I and my parents could only send flowers to the funeral home.

Resolvement-- Molly Sullivan told my parents that Dr. Davis has recommended further evaluations and I should contact you about what I should do. I am now contacting you to find out what would be the best approach. Obviously, conducting evaluations in Orlando would be more conducive logistically, but I will do them where ever you think it would better serve me in getting the visitation I deeply desire. I look forward to hearing your guidance in this matter and look forward to a speedy end to this alienation. It has been over six months since I have seen my children and I fear I am losing touch with them. If you feel this letter should be shared with Molly Sullivan, please feel free to allow her to read it.

Thank you in advance,
Nathan J. Isbell

October 26, 2006
To: Jerry Pilgrim Esquire
From: Nathan J. Isbell
Re: Questions for (1st Wife) during trial

- She claims abandonment. During deposition, Grady asked a series of questions about why she did not go to Atlanta to check on me. She claims she feared for the children and her own safety. Why would I stay in the household when she was afraid of me? She also claims the vehicle she was driving for the past three weeks was unreliable, I had driven this vehicle extensively. Then she admits the air-conditioning had stopped working. Why would she truly not go to Atlanta to check on her husband of 19 years, that she stated under oath was a good husband, good provider, good father and was only exhibiting, in her words, that I was acting in a radical behavior?

During deposition, Grady asked her if she had told me that her parents told her that they were not leaving any inheritance to her due to their fear that I would use the money to pay off my parents. Her answer was that she did not recall. This was a yes or no question. Why would she have to even think about this if it wasn't true?

She has a possible boyfriend that resides in the near proximity of her family's condo in Florida. He is involved with real estate. Broker or agent? Why would she get a Florida Real Estate license and then have it transferred to Alabama, was she planning to relocate? In the two years of our separation, she had a part-time job that lasted for approximately 3 months and just recently got her real estate license in 2006, if she was in such dire straits financially, why would she go for a career that is straight commission? When asked to get a job to help with our family before the separation, it was not even an option. How is it now an option?

As many times as Nathan has told you about his bleak financial situation, his requests for you to get a job to help support the family, the loss of his business and furthermore even his now discharged bankruptcy, why would you think he has somehow managed to acquire the resources to still support the lifestyle the two of you were living?

Is it true that Lauren wishes to have absolutely no contact with her father? Why do you think she doesn't? Have you ever heard of what is called P. A. S. or Parental Alienation Syndrome? Do you think the conversations that you have had with your daughter over the past two years would fall into that proven category? Is it also true that Lauren has requested to not have any contact with her grandparents. Even going as far as writing them a letter returning their Christmas gift that was in the form of a check and referring to it as pity money? Nathan said you have always referred to his parent's generosity and love as being on their pity pot. Could this be where a 15-year-old girl would get terms such as pity money?

Nathan has been putting monies into a custodian account for the children with Edward Jones investments since the time of separation. He claims that you wanted to have the account set up where he had no access giving control over to a Trustee, why? She had told me she didn't want me to drain the account like I had done with the accounts that my parents had set up. She also told my kids that they would never see any of this money in these accounts, because I had drained them before and I would do it again. The truth is, the accounts were closed to get enough money to pay off the tax lien that I was unaware of, so we could qualify for the loan on the McGregor Court house that she had to have. She was fully aware of this, but the kids didn't get the whole story. Thus damaging my credibility for what I am trying to do for them for the future. Is this Parental Alienation Syndrome?

When her father was admitted to the hospital in (City) Georgia and there were several times. She only visited one time after repeated offers from my parents to assist with the children. Why did she only visit one time and why did she stay only one day before going to the family condo at the beach for the next three days? Couldn't she have been of more service to her mother and father in their time of need?

(1st Wife)'s bank statements reflect deposits into her account of approximately $109,000. During that period of January 2005 through October 2005. This works out to $10,900 per month. Where did this much money come from and why did she require so much?

(1st Wife)'s ability to keep a clean house was terrible, even with a housekeeper weekly. The housekeeper even told (1st Wife) to keep up with the cleaning during the interim of the weekly visits, which angered (1st Wife). How is it that a full-time mom utilizing all available Moms Day Out programs when the children were young and of course full-time school later, would fail at keeping a clean house? What did she do all day?

What was the reason for becoming so discontent with a house in a wonderful subdivisions such as Leesburg located on Knollwood Drive? We spruced the house up with new hardwood flooring throughout and new ceramic tile in the kitchen. It was 2600 ft.^{2}, the same as the house on McGregor Court. We had new furnishings throughout, yet she still was discontent. Her major complaint was that it was 20 minutes away from all of the activities in Spring Hill. Was this really enough of a hardship to warrant moving to the Spring Hill area when our finances were on the verge of ruin?

(1st Wife) would spend hours on the phone gossiping with her friends even after I had repeatedly warned her about doing this. Austin is not a self motivated child with his homework and every time that I spent time with him, he scores well. (1st Wife) had wanted to put Austin on medication for years and I resisted. She almost instantly had it prescribed after the separation. Does she think that a little less telephone time would be better directed towards Austin's homework efforts to alleviate his need for prescribed drugs?

Due to the many phone conversations with (1st Wife) calling me names, I requested that all future contact be made via e-mail. She strongly denied this request. She does not want to give up the pleasure she gains from humiliating me? Or is it that she doesn't want a form of written contact available for the record?

LETTER TO:

WHOM IT MAY CONCERN

March 20, 2006

To Whom it May Concern:

This illustration of the LEGACY TRUST is based on life insurance, but can just as easily be set up from liquid cash. The LEGACY TRUST can be set up in many other ways as well. I had even thought of all qualified recipients are required to have a family health coverage plan, otherwise the LEGACY checks would be applied to the premium and whatever was left over sent to the heir. This is just one of many applications. The LEGACY plan can be introduced via an infomercial informing the public of a website that they can go to and set this up online or order an info package. I noticed a website selling a do it yourself living Will for $149.95 just fill in the blanks. With a modest cost far below what an attorney would charge, they can set up a LEGACY TRUST of their very own. Insurance salespeople can present it as part of their sales package. They can ask their client the all too familiar question "Who do you want the beneficiary to be?". When so many people are aware that the money will be short-lived and they will be forgotten. Or they can ask the client if they would like to leave a LEGACY TRUST to all their heirs for an eternity. This is truly their chance to make a difference in this world before they go to meet their maker.

By not trying to convert existing policyholders like A. L. Williams did in the 80's, but trying to add additional benefits to existing and or new policies. The big insurance companies will not want to squash the idea, but may embrace it as a valuable tool in selling their own policies. If it can be patented it wouldn't matter. We still get paid.

Depending on the initial installment and the number of qualified recipients, the size of the LEGACY checks will vary.

But taking into consideration the rule of 72's where based on the rate of return divided into 72 determines how many years before your money doubles, these LEGACY checks can get very sizable. For instance, a $1 million policy as illustrated. 500,000 goes toward the relief of immediate family matters. The remaining $500,000 gets put into an investment account of choice. Let's just say the broker can average you a conservative 10%. That means 5% or $25,000 will be paid out to the registered heirs and $25,000 will be reinvested. Using simple math and the rule of 72's 10/72 equals 7.2 in 7.2 years their money will double, but we are paying out 50% so it will take 14.4 years to double. If each recipient isn't entitled to participate until their 18th birthday, this will enable the fund to escalate to the point of a sizable check for each recipient. I'm not going to take the time to show you the power of compounded interest, but I hope you get the point. More importantly, the masses of people that would love to leave their mark for an eternity and for all of their future generations to enjoy, get the point. Giving thanks to that one person that took the time and interest to set it up. Your name will live forever.

May GOD bless,

Nathan J. Isbell

LETTER TO:

JO BONNER
U.S. CONGRESSMAN

DISCRIMINATION
IN PUBLIC SCHOOLS

These are notes sent home by the teachers of my stepson Chase.

1. Said "shut up Ms. Snowden"
2. acting on playing an air guitar during spelling
3. talk to family

I'm going to let you give Chase his conduct grade.

Ms. Snowden

Chase is a bright kid who is going to waste away his education. Please tell him the importance.
Thanks,
Mr. Avera

Mr. Avera,

I am on your side. I tell both of my children how important education is to their future. However, I am not Chase's teacher. I was not in the classroom yesterday. I feel that it is your job to give him the letter that he deserves.

Chase came home and told me that you would not allow him to get some tissue to blow his nose, and he said he had to wipe his nose with his hand. He also said that you or some aide called him lazy in front of the entire class. I am not a child psychologist, but that is pretty 101 to know not to ridicule children in front of other people. If that is how you are treating Chase, he will always meet those goals. If you give him the slightest encouragement, he listens and he wants to please.

Chase is punished because of his "U" on Monday and because of yesterday, but remember, you can feed life into him or death, you choose what you want to.

(2nd Wife)

Please call me. I called you on Friday.

To:Jo Bonner US Congressman
11 N. Water Street Suite 15290
Mobile, AL 36602

From: Nathan J. Isbell
P.O. Box 1371
Gulf Shores, AL 36547
e-mail – nathanjisbell@yahoo.com
cell phone – 251 – XXX – XXXX

Dear Mr. Bonner,

I have unfortunately discovered discrimination in our public school system concerning mental health. My son is a student at UMS-Wright and his ADHD was detected by a teacher that was obviously trained how to detect this disorder. He has received the proper medication and is able to function socially as well as academically. My stepson is a student at Foley Intermediate and he exemplifies many of the characteristics of a child with ADD. After a conference with his teacher and principal, I became very alarmed by their statements. I asked them if the teachers were to take it upon themselves to be educated in the symptoms of children with ADD/ADHD what would happen? They are instructed by the Principle not to inform the child's parents due to the financial liability that would be incurred by the Federal Government. This statement coincides with the statements of the former U.S. Surgeon General David Satcher M.D. He states that African Americans are not privileged the medical access that white children are afforded. From my vantage point, not only is the African-American child not receiving the medical attention he needs to become a productive member of society, he is being Govern-mentally suppressed due to finances.

In closing, I'm not interested in playing the blame game. I just want to hear some viable solutions to fix the problem at hand.

Concerned parent,
Nathan J. Isbell

LETTER TO:

PASTOR RICK LONG AND ELDERS

CHRISTIAN LIFE CHURCH ORANGE BCH, ALABAMA

Do We Fit In?

Dear Rick and Elders,

On September 2, 2006 at the end of the service, you gave a heart-wrenching plea to the church to be mature and understanding. Stating that although you do not condone this behavior, you asked that it be addressed and forgiven. My first thoughts were that you yourself had engaged in a sinful act and felt compelled to publicly ask for forgiveness. I sat completely ready to hear your confession and have forgiveness and not judgment in my heart. To my surprise, the public address was not concerning you, but members of your congregation. As you proceed with this story the couple in question boldly walked to the front of the church as if it were orchestrated and this was their way of cleansing their hearts with a public confession. I did not know how to react, but to be stunned as I think many others were. I left church that day with a feeling of compassion and empathy for what they and their families would face by their decisions. I knew they asked for forgiveness and by the grace of GOD, they shall receive it. I prayed for them and didn't think that much about it, for I do not know them and my life was not effected. It later came to my attention via a friend, that this public confession was in fact not orchestrated and came as a complete shock to them. I have to admire their strength to face the church and silently say, “Ye without sin cast the first stone”. Especially to address a congregation that you all to often refer to as a trophy shelf of undesirables.

You may be wondering at this point that if I don't know them, why I feel so strongly about this issue. The fact is that I'm trying to finalize a divorce of a 21 year marriage that's started September 2004 and hopefully will be resolved in January 2007. This in and of itself is not the crux of the matter, the events after the breakup are. But first, a little about me. I had not been raised a Christian do to my parent's decision to stop attending while I was very young. At the time it didn't bother me because church didn't do anything but interfere with my weekend play activities. I've since asked my mother why we stopped attending and her reply was that the people there were more interested in gossip sessions than praising the Lord. We were a family of meager means and she was sure that we were the subject of conversation when we were not present.

Probably four years ago, I started to attend the church that I had officially belong to for the last 12 years. I attended as a means to free myself from the company of my spouse for a few short hours, for I knew that she wouldn't attend. Somewhere along the way I decided to pay attention and see what all the hub bub was about. My knowledge of the Bible was minimal at best and I chose to remain silent in Sunday school, so as not to reveal my ignorance on the subject. I got caught up in the word and found myself looking forward to going on Sunday. At the point of my absolute hit the bottom turmoil, I began to write down my thoughts. I really felt like GOD and I were connecting on a level that completely astonished me. I knew who to turn to, to discuss my revelation. So I went to my minister. It seemed the right thing to do, he's always up front saying “Come, Come”. So I went and it became one of the biggest mistakes of my life. I turned over all my written documents to him to read and later call me to discuss. When I called him, I found that he had only read a few of the first pages and he thought I was trying to get him to invest in something. After he did read my most personal thoughts I gave to him in confidence, he then turned them over to my wife. These documents enabled her to receive a restraining order, separation from my children for seven months and only supervised visitation after that, until I completed a series of psychological evaluations that lasted almost a full year. All to prove that I was not insane and not a threat to my children. (of course I was cleared of all these allegations). Between what I received and what this couple received, I think that I would opt for the public humiliation. My TRUST for organized religion was history, but my personal relationship with GOD flourished

After spending a full year not allowing myself the pleasure of a relationship, I met what I feel like today is my soul mate. She too had experienced extreme let downs with organized religion and could totally relate to what I had experienced. After her divorce and realization that it was up to her and the help of GOD to pick herself up and raise two children on her own, she isolated herself for five years. When she decided that it was time to give herself the chance to live again with the comforts of a partner, her biggest concern with this partner was that he be a Godly Man. She met what she thought was such a person that portrayed himself in a Godly manner, only to find out later that unfortunately it was deception. The man had been separated from his wife for 18 months and due to the lengthy divorce proceedings had not officially closed the divorce. Upon this information surfacing to the church that they all attended, including his soon-to-be ex, she was ostracized and asked not to return. She respectfully bowed out and chose another church. Fortunately, she did not allow someone that positions himself as judge and jury to diminish her faith in GOD.

Immediately after I started dating her, she started to try to return me to a place of TRUST. Christian Life Church seemed to be this place. A place where us undesirables could come and worship without fear of being ostracized. I had even told her that I was compelled to make a public confession of faith and tell the story of how materialism destroyed the second quarter of my life. I'm glad I didn't do that. Just GOD and I and of course my new found soul mate. During my new friends transition to another church, she did confide in the new minister. She told me that he made a very profound statement. “Churches are the only army I know that shoot their wounded.” Somehow we are expected to be held to a higher standard after receiving the Lord Jesus Christ as our Savior, when the fact is that we are still human and we will commit sins of the flesh.

We will continue attending Christian Life Church because we love it and connect with GOD every week. We are fully aware that any Minister is nothing more than a man, an instrument of GOD revealing the word and quite capable of committing sins of the flesh themselves and should not consider themselves judge and jury over his disciples. So with all of this said,

Do We Fit In?

Nathan J. Isbell (2nd Wife)

LETTER TO:

FORREST AND KATHY

October 1, 2007

Dear Forest and Kathy,

My life has changed so much in the last three years. Now that the dust is beginning to settle, I have time to reflect on my thoughts and my purpose for GOD. The reason that I am contacting you is because you are the only one from the church to make unsolicited contact with me. "Nothing just happens" T. D. Jakes. I found it interesting that you were unaware of the goings on with (1st Wife) and I and were merely inquiring about a future business transaction. Not until you informed me, were you informed about the I'm sure juicy gossip. But as I attempt to fulfill my purpose, I met with roadblock after roadblock. This morning as I lie in bed restless, the Lord reminds me that the only person to contact me was a lawyer and a Godly man. I am writing you today, to solicit your help accomplishing this mission that leaves me with no rest.

I believe I have a solution for a lot of issues that remain unresolved. The politicians continually scratched around it, but haven't found it. This can be observed in the Sunday paper headline "Clinton idea of $5000 for babies has critics smelling political blood". Wow, is this what our society has become. If someone is thinking out loud for the purpose of the betterment of our future generations, why are they subject to such ridicule? Although, I am not interested in increasing my taxes to afford these programs, I am however very interested in fixing the dilemma at hand. Social Security, health care and the Baby Boom Generation 401(k) plans that are scheduled to start maturing in the year 2010.

LEGACY TRUST is a concept that may not be the panacea, but it certainly couldn't hurt. As people that have life insurance die, they have policies to benefit the ones that they love with immediate cash gratification. Some people even have the financial intelligence to use this windfall to establish themselves a nice income producing asset column on their financial statement. Most do not know what a financial statement is. As parents, we are always trying to teach our children morality and ethics, but we ourselves were never trained the learned skill of financial intelligence. This is a mission that people like Robert Kiyosaki , author of the Rich Dad series of books, have felt called to accomplish. With all of the success Robert enjoys, he is only able to reach a very small, but growing number of people that are not just thinkers, but doers. Most will continue to rely on the government to be the safety net for all of their needs. As my wife's icon Bishop TD Jakes would recommend, “It is time that we begin thinking Generationally”.

The first obstacle to overcome was the perpetuity laws that exist. Upon death, the life insurance will have execution instructions to wire benefits to a LEGACY TRUST held by the financial planner the policyholder has selected as Trustee. The Trustee will then disburse these benefits as the policyholder has inputted online or otherwise. The selections can be changed up until the time of death since no disbursements will occur until then. After the traditional immediate cash gratification and burial arrangements are taken care of, the remaining percentage of benefits will be placed in its own LLC. This LLC will be in the control of the Trustee and invested into the US stock exchange. After a 50% reinvest, the remaining 50% can be disbursed in the form of LEGACY checks. The disbursement and frequency of these checks will be dictated by the policyholder using the scroll down selection process on the website. One of the scrolls will ask for a corporate name. This corporate name will appear on all checks and can be anything non-vulgar the policyholder wants for all of his heirs to remember him by. All people that are direct descendents of the policyholder are entitled to an equal variable share in the LLC disbursements at age 18 and all charitable organizations are assigned a set percentage.

Governmental involvement would be great to facilitate a lower tax on this new found income stream, possibly 15% like the capital gains tax. And if this money could somehow be directed to Social Security to take care of the most I was speaking of earlier. This cost the taxpayer zero dollars and will inevitably reduce the tax burden we all face.

The LEGACY TRUST website will be a simple easy-to-follow, step-by-step process that will enable policyholders to convert their existing beneficiaries to a LEGACY TRUST online. The cost to the consumers will be zero dollars and they can establish a LEGACY TRUST of their own. Leaving their mark for an eternity. All financial planners will be listed on the scroll downs leaving the choice to the policyholder. The financial planning institutions will pay a royalty on my patent based on new conversions, sales and financial planning.

I could never spend the kind of money that this patented idea will generate, so I will trade places with GOD. I'll take 10% and open him a LEGACY TRUST account with the 90% solely geared for the socialization of FREE medical care. People should have the right to healthcare at no mandatory cost and people should have the right to pay for healthcare if they deem it as a better value. The country that I serve believes in capitalism and is struggling with the connection with socialized healthcare. Maybe one day GOD's LEGACY TRUST LLC will pay out enough in payroll to attract the best physicians available.

The 401(k) crisis is on the horizon. The first wave of government mandated absolute sell offs of the baby boom generations retirement fund begins in 2010. How many waves of sell off's can the market stand before there is a rush to salvage what is left of people's nest eggs. When people are 80 years old and a crash hits the market, will their financial plan work? How long of a recovery can they stand? GOD's LEGACY TRUST LLC will buy all their shares and allow people to retire to the coast and fulfill all their retirement dreams. I give full credit for this 401(k) crisis prediction to Robert Kiyosaki's Rich Dad. Refer to his book Prophecy.

Forrest, I need you to write up this TRUST in a legal fashion so that it can be presented to the US patent office. I will pay you for your services. I hope what you have read reveals my heart and you will take it upon yourself to help me finish this mission giving GOD the glory.

Thank you in advance and GOD bless,
Nathan J. Isbell

LETTER TO:

WHOM IT MAY TOUCH

To Whom it May Touch:

I worry about my retirement. I worry about the baby boom generation reaching retirement. I worry if their 401(k) plans will produce all they were promised. I worry about the year 2010 when the boomers start to retire. I worry if at 70 ½ when they must start receiving installments from their stocks, will there be enough buyers to keep the stock price up. I worry if there will be enough buyers to sustain the barrage of boomers that will be forced to sell for the many years to come. I worry about my parents generation, where their employers guarantee pensions till death. I'm worried about these novice investors that were only really given one viable option to plan for their futures. I worry they will not listen to the advice of savvy investors that try and convince them to keep their money in the market, it will be okay, it's only your life savings. I worry that if we get into a bear market reducing their nest eggs, they will be looking to cash in early and I can only pray that this doesn't spark a crash where hard-working people settle for pennies on the dollar and are forced to return to the workforce, instead of enjoying their golden years.

I wonder if anyone has come up with a fix to this potentially dangerous scenario? I wonder if anyone would be interested in a possible fix? I wonder if at the time a life insurance policy beneficiary section were to be filled out and an option of the LEGACY TRUST was offered, I wonder if people might prefer to give an inheritance to their offspring for an eternity? I wonder if anyone that has children that can't seem to manage money, if they would feel comfortable that a LEGACY TRUST will at a minimum provide health insurance? I wonder if people would like the convenience of buying a life insurance policy/Will and TRUST and have their life long efforts spread out into monthly dividend checks that are distributed to all qualified members equally? I wonder if anyone would like to buy or even convert their existing policy to a LEGACY TRUST? I would but this product, but it is not available so I'm having to spend $450 in legal fees and all the brainstorming I can handle to set something up at the time of my death. I want all of my heirs to receive a monthly check with an encouraging note from me. I wonder if other people would like to leave their mark in this world? I wonder if the amount of insurance settlements deposited into the marketplace will be enough to absorb the barrage of absolute SELLERS keeping their stock prices high so their 401k plans will work? I wonder if anyone even with meager means, would like to leave a LEGACY TRUST to a charitable group or church, you could certainly make up some ground on tithing? I wonder if anyone will be touched by this concept and will take it to the next level? I wonder when we will address this coming potential crisis? I wonder if we can pay the debt left by US and from previous generations and not pass it on to future generations? I wonder if people can see past their immediate greed and see the benefit of receiving their birthrights over time? I wonder if my Savior is satisfied with my efforts?

Nathan J. Isbell

LETTER TO:

MR. DAVID WALKER

FORMER U.S. COMPTROLLER

11-5-2007
To: David Walker U. S. Comptroller
Government Accountability Office
441 G. St. N. W.
Washington, DC. 20548

From: Nathan J. Isbell
P.O. Box 1371
Gulf Shores, AL 36547

Dear Mr. Walker,

The concept of the fiscal wake up tour is designed to draw from individual citizens an idea that will solve the "Financial Implosion" that is on the horizon. You say in your statement(USA Today 10/9/2007) the problem stems from "the power of compounding". Ironically, the solution is derived from the same statement. The answer is compounded interest.

Rebuild Social Security

Allow taxpayers to use their death benefits to open an LLC. This LLC will be invested into the US stock exchange. The monthly yield will be reinvested 50% and 50% distributed to the taxpayers heirs and or charities. This creates a new found, never ending taxable income stream that can be channeled to rebuild Social Security.

Global issues/Emergency Funds/Charities

Illustration Purposes only:

We are the World Campaign
Total collected? $10 million
Year collected? 1985
Average annual interest collected? 10%

Compounded interest has always amazed us, this is how we can put it to work for us and the rest of the world.

Year	**balance after 5% reinvest**	**5% disbursement**
1986	10,500,000	500,000
1987	11,025,000	551,250
1988	11,576,250	578,812
1989	12,155,062	607,753
1990	12,762,815	638,140
1991	13,400,955	670,047
1992	14,071,002	703,550
1993	14,774,552	738,727
1994	15,513,279	775,663
1995	16,288,942	814,447
1996	17,103,389	855,169
1997	17,958,558	897,927
1998	18,856,485	942,824
1999	19,799,309	989,965
2000	20,789,274	1,039,463
	rule of 72's 72/5% = 14.4 years	
2001	21,828,737	1,091,436
2002	22,920,173	1,146,008
2003	24,066,181	1,203,309
2004	25,269,490	1,263,474
2005	26,532,964	1,326,648
2006	27,859,612	1,392,980
2007	29,252,592	1,462,629
2008	30,715,221	1,535,761
Total	**$21,725,982**	

If in 1985 $10 million was collected and put into a Feed the World LEGACY TRUST yielding 10%. The total disbursed funds since 1985 would be $21,725,982 and the annual disbursement would be $1,535,761 for the year 2008. This would cost the taxpayer absolutely zero dollars. Feel free to add as many zeros as you would like. That's a lot of rice.

<u>Socialized medical care</u>

Patented royalties paid by life insurance companies and financial planning institutions will fund this LEGACY TRUST. Private healthcare will be unaffected, but the uninsured can receive healthcare for free, costing the taxpayer $0.

This is a crude example of the future LEGACY TRUST website/written applications: anything underlined is a variable scroll down option.

LEGACY TRUST

Leave your mark for an Eternity

At the time of my death, please disburse <u>50%</u> Of my total death benefit as the immediate cash funds to the following beneficiaries.

Spouse	<u>50%</u>
Child	<u>25%</u>
Child	<u>25%</u>

The remaining <u>50%</u> Of my total death benefit is to be put in TRUST with <u>Edward Jones investments.</u>

Edward Jones investments will establish an LLC with all qualified recipients as equal variable shareholders. Your corporate name for your LEGACY TRUST will be printed on every LEGACY check that your heirs will receive. <u>In 25 words</u>

or less write what you want all of your future bloodline to see on their check. Subject to approval.

This LLC will send all qualified recipients an equal Monthly LEGACY check.

After a 50% Reinvest LEGACY checks to be disbursed as follows:

Qualified Recipients	90%
Home of Grace-- Vancleave Ms	5%
Youth Reach – Elberta Al	5%

Rules and Regulations for Qualified Recipients

- must register with investment broker 30 days prior to each birthday with proof of lineage and birth certificate
- no liens may be attached
- No back payments
- organizations that fail to register within three years will be deleted and proceeds to go into qualified recipient funds
- if investment brokers fees are excessive or the rate of return falls below 10% For 2 Years in the last 5 Years, a majority vote of qualified recipients may change investment brokers to a different legitimate broker under preset guidelines. Tie No Change
- minimum LEGACY check is $100 after fees and expenses, otherwise account will reinvest 100% until this can occur
- only direct bloodline lineage qualifies, no extended families
- spouse of qualified recipients Does Qualify as my replacement upon my death

- must register all births of your bloodline within first year, income stream may Not Be sold for one Lump sum. Both of these infractions risk losing your shares at a majority vote. Tie No.
- Fund must have a positive yield or there will be no LEGACY check for that period

In closing, the love of money may be the root of all evil, but it can sure solve a lot of problems today and in the future. The possibilities of this plan are endless.

May GOD Bless America and the rest of the World,
Nathan J. Isbell

CC: Jo Bonner US Congressman
Bill O'Reilly Fox News
Harry Zeeve Concorde Coalition
Rush Limbaugh

SECOND MANIC EPISODE

THE CRAZY STUFF

I AM

I AM contacting you now.
Is Help really on the way?
Check out the front page of USA Today October 9, 2007
I have the remedy.
I am ready.

666 – important dates?

Riddles:
27 coins
What happened to the other dollar?
Two men Two doors
Larry's son

I am gay – Kevin Kline

If I could just get some bottom land – Sgt. York
I figured those guns were killing hundreds, maybe thousands, so I had to stop them guns.

After Sgt. York got what he wanted, I heard he returned back to the bottle.

You sure learned a lot up in those hills Alvin.

It must be nice to always think you're the smartest one in the room – Broadcast News

If you could express yourself right now, I know that you would do a better job than I – Hook

Simba, you are more than you have become – Lion King

Young lady / Old lady – Shallow Hal

Fire, Fire, Look at what I have created – Castaway

World Peace – Miss Congeniality

Loaded gun – There's something about Mary

Rape, Pedophile, Institutionalize – Shawshank Redemption

Republicans and Democrats – Heat Miser and Mr. Freeze

Island of Misfit Toys – Lepers

I wish I had $1 million – It's a Wonderful Life

My people want freedom/HEALTHCARE and I go to see that they have it – Braveheart

You make me want to be a better man – As GOD as it Gets

You complete me – Jerry Maguire

Scooby Doo ending – Wayne's world

Fake charities – The Jerk

Ability to smell an ambush – Braveheart

Run for it Marty – Back to the Future

Opinions are like assholes, we all got one – Platoon
Two camps – Hate and Love

Turkish prison – Pain, Guilt, Customs, Cultures, Homecoming – Midnight Express

Golden goose – Jack and the Beanstalk

Fame – Failure - Rebirth and Wiser – Rock Star

Wizard of Oz – TD Jakes
Will work for food

666 # of a man?

Get your credit score up to 666 and you have a right of passage as a man
Rituals – Roots

Betrayal – Patrick and Terry

The Two Headed Beast is what holds us captive, it can be slayed. This is the struggle that every Man contends with. - Restraint

The market needs more money for continuity. GOD's LEGACY TRUST LLC will create a new foundation.

Real-life knowledge – Back-to-School Rodney Dangerfield

Lower-priced tuna, That's American man. Schooner tuna, the tuna with a heart. – Mr. Mom

If our country was a football team, would you say we're having a winning season? – Heaven Can Wait

We don't care what the other teams are doing, we want to do the right thing. If the porpoises are getting caught in the nets, we'll charge an extra penny per can to save them. We'll be on the porpoise team. We'll advertise "Would you pay an extra penny to save the fish that thinks?"

I want it now daddy – Willy Wonka and the Chocolate Factory
Impatient – No Discipline – No Guidance – Uneducated - Greed

Hold up signs during clips like Wayne's world, cool

I was rushed through my mortgage closing – Ignorance

Do you know how easy this is for me? – Good Will Hunting

Stay free mini pad joke

Build businesses for the lepers and halfway houses.
Hope of going home serving humble pie
Pie – Michael

He smells like cookies – Michael – vanity

What do you do when your real-life exceeds your dreams?
Keep it to yourself – Broadcast News
Corruption brought on by Envy

I was saving up for a Husband – It's a Wonderful Life
Generosity – Compassion – Racism

I've got a Golden ticket – LEGACY Will and TRUST – Willy Wonka

Feed tuna mayonnaise – Night Shift
Creativity – realized failure - QUIT
How much will it cost your family?
Bipolar disorder
How much does it cost us, to not let you create?

Would you hire a leper?
Let's all take our masks off and put on a new one
Mask – Jim Carrey

Funny how when he puts on the Mask, the real person inside emerges. Is this what intoxicants do? Hows that working out for you?

Anyone who challenges
You're going to lose – A League of their Own

Let me just stop you right there, before you say something you will inevitably regret – You've got Mail

That's the gift that keeps on giving – Christmas Vacation
LEGACY Will and TRUST

Not everyone thinks like you Patrice.
Oh yes they do, they just don't admit it. – Coming to America
Narrow Minded – No understanding of Cultural Diversities

We must be getting close, I'm getting a hard on – Top Gun

October 16, 2007

Financial Intelligence Required

Before I except my clinical bipolar diagnosis, take my meds, suppress my creativity and slip into a lethargic state like the rest of the kids on Ritalin. I would like someone with financial intelligence to tell me why this won't work.

Will someone please answer these questions? Can LEGACY Will and TRUST: feed the world - stop drug abuse with quarterly screenings for non-prescribed medication - keep the stock market from crashing – Answer my 11-year-old stepson's birthday wish to bring prayer back to schools – show the world we want peace through the teachings of Jesus Christ – not to mention a check from GOD's LEGACY TRUST for their daily bread – profile everyone that wants free services – such as healthcare and food – will this help to stop terrorism by knowing who is here?

Cut through all of the political spin? Start healing people on the inside with mental counseling? Why did the 14-year-old kill himself for GOD? Did his teachings from home not match society? Put GOD back into our hearts? Change foreign perception of the United States and GOD. If not the present generation, possibly the future generations that are receiving LEGACY checks from GOD? Stop civil liberties unions from pandering to the sensitivities of other cultures and beliefs, while sacrificing what my forefathers fought for? Stop global warming? Just kidding or am I. Put your money where your mouth is. Let everyone know that GOD loves us so much he sent his only son to save us. We crucified him and it set us on the wrong path? Set us on GOD's path?

Anonymous Christian/African-American

Set up a global warming TRUST fund, so I don't have to pay for you to chase rabbits.
Don't you dare ask Caesar for another red cent.

I worked real hard for this Louie – Trading Places
TRUST

Movie – kids get wrapped up in their class instructor while he was illustrating how easy Hitler had it. Can we rally behind GOD? The insignia for GOD's LEGACY TRUST LLC means healing. Red Cross – Jesus has left, but the blood remains. Gold and Purple Serpent – Temptations – Sin

Escape – Indian – One who flew over the cuckoo's nest

Let Caesar have what is Caesar's
15% Federal 5% State
Let GOD have what belongs to GOD 10%

I did not want to bore you with numbers again, I was looking at the $10 million illustration for the starving children in Africa. It says, if in 1985 $10 million was collected and put into a feed the world LEGACY TRUST fund yielding 10% annually, the African 2008 Rice budget would be in excess of 1.5 million that costs the taxpayer zero dollars. That's a lot of rice that we didn't have to ask for a donation for.

After the $10 million was spent and not invested back in 1985, what is the Rice budget today? How are we going to pay it so people don't starve? What better way to stop the war on terrorism, than by winning their hearts through their stomachs. Win with love.

How much does the Jerry Lewis telethon fund have in their account? How much would their Rice budget be? Or will we need another boring Telethon to feed today's need.

How many examples of how GOD's LEGACY plan works do you need? Money may be the root of all evil, but it can solve a lot of problems. When your money works for all of us, rather than us working for money. At present, we spend more than we have and the marketplace has caught up with us. Can we leave our future generations a bill or a check. The time for change is now. Or we could just leave it to our dogs. I can only hope they have more financial intelligence than the current recipients.

When the government pension plans go bankrupt, will that wake us up? Probably not, that generation will be dead.

October 30, 2007

To: David Walker
Re: Fiscal Wake Up Tour Challenge

The answer is compounded interest. In lieu of increasing the inheritance tax, allow taxpayers to use their death benefits to open an LLC. This LLC will be invested into the US stock exchange. The monthly yield will be reinvested 50% and 50% disbursed to the taxpayers heirs. This creates a new found income stream that can be taxed forever.

Our arrogance makes us think it is trying to communicate with us – Star Trek IV
Cultural Diversity-- Ego

Such Decadence – Moscow on the Hudson

Happy learned how to putt – Happy Gilmore
Focus – write what I want to say

Exchange info for a transfer – A Few Good Men
Discrimination for LEGACY

Problem first – Discrimination
Solutions second

Drawing for a month-long cruise, one ticket per person, one dollar. That is your permanent number, maybe this is the number you need to get goods and services or this is the antichrist. I don't want to be the antichrist.

You don't tug on Superman's cape. You don't piss into the wind. You don't pull, the mask off the Lone Ranger and you don't mess around with HIM – Jim Croce

I don't know who I am
I don't know who I am supposed to be
I do know, I am more than I have become. – Lion King

I am on the verge of a nervous breakdown.
Without a backup plan and GOD to talk to, I cringe.
Would prescribed medication erase the line of reality and cause me to do something I ordinarily wouldn't do? I think so.

Hold on, wait a minute, let me put some GOD in it. Ooh Aah

If this plan doesn't work, I am as crazy as a run over dog. Check me in. No prescribed meds please. On second thought, I'll have the buffet.

I feel your pain – Million Dollar Baby
Parental Alienation Syndrome

Anyone willing to give up birthrights for one lump sum. I want to know what he is going to do with the money. He may be a prophet.

Special Ed is for Goofy screws – Island of Misfit Toys

The Starving will Sing
Rub a Dub Dub
Thanks for the Grub
Yeah GOD!!!

A horny man is a dangerous thing – History Channel

Men can not be Trusted to adopt. Heterosexuals have a hard enough time restraining from perversion. Homosexuals will cross the line of morality and a child should not be subject to such. Lesbians can procreate on their own during a one night stand, but their perverted make up is totally different than a mans and I believe they make fine nurturing mothers. Neither should be allowed to adopt.

I ask our father time to fix problems. Give me the strength to make them heed.

Do you want Hank? – Me, Myself and Irene
Vulgarity – Two personalities – Good and Evil – Angel and Devil

Exercise the Demon – Pet Detective
I know I am right!!!

Sean Hannity is the Heat Miser
Alan Combs is Mr. Freeze

Bill O'Reilly – I am too much.

All I am saying
Is give peace a chance – Billy Jack

I love the girl that screams out obscenities, so he takes her to a ballgame – Deuce Bigelow Male Gigolo
She gets your attention, doesn't she? Does GOD need to scream out obscenities to get your attention?

Is it too much to ask for a roof over your head and food to eat – George Bailey
Anyway my father didn't think so.

Is it too much to ask for free medical care? – Nathan

We are Hungry
Are we Worthy
Before the Word Thy GOD

Thank you for my Mother and Dad.
You did real good Momma—Forrest Gump
He made his peace with GOD – Lieut. Dan

It is hard to chill, when the devil blocks my purpose.

All things are possible for those that believe in our GOD through Jesus Christ, his only begotten son.

My title is Wonderful Counselor for I serve a Wonderful GOD!

Lord, please do not lead me to temptation. Cleanse my soul.

I'm not worthy – Wayne's world

Self-Esteem – Weird Science

Bumper stickers:
Are you following Jesus this close?
Normal people frighten me
On Fire for GOD

That's the thing about that line, they keep moving that little sucker – Broadcast News

The Line of Reality – Over prescribed medication

I have learned shorthand with my Aletheia.
I can bring a whole story to you from a small clip of a movie. I have the ability to draw from movie clips, the answer for most quandaries and direction of how I want to take my own life. Are the movies that are being produced today, exemplifying the message that we want our children to lead their lives by?

I'll be home for Christmas, if only in my dreams.

I am Jim – Taxi
Aletheia

You want me on that wall
You need me on that wall
You want TRUTH
You can't handle the truth – A Few Good Men

My name is Sue Seer.
Excuse me, what is your name?

Her name is Lucille – Volunteers
Dialect – Speaking in Tongues
not Yibbity Yibbity Yah Yah Yah Praise GOD – Can I get a A-A-A-AMEN!!!

Once Solomon gained all the wisdom. He gained all the greed and lusts of this world. He made a mistake.

What have you learned Dorothy?-- Wizard of Oz

Acts 17:31 I don't want to pick a date

1 Thessalonians 1 – 5

Hebrews 10:27 give me the faith that will seal my salvation, Lord
please Lord

Matthew 24:40 I have been warned

So shall it be written, So shall it be done – the 10 Commandments

2 Thess 2:1-4 Jesus has got my back
1 Tim 4:1-2 everybody's got their own agenda
2 Peter 2:1 – 3 not a good job to be in, if your heart is not right with GOD

Wooganowski-- Duh Woogie – There's something about Mary
Nathan – Duh Nathan the Prophet

Knowledge of Nathan – ask Gene

Only pierced never a broken bone,
I remember that proclamation.
What a dumb ass AM I.

Know your place, he that would sit at the front, shall sit at the back.

I will build your temple, Lord
Not filled with the riches of Solomon
But filled with the technology of this culture. Here we will use it and beat the devil at his own game – Media
Your temple will be called Leper Land
Your Grace will heal your people
Faith – Always Been, Always Be

But what about graduation?

When you can take pebble from my hand, time for you to leave – Kung Fu

Wow, how naive
We need a halfway house
Roof – Food – Clothing – Medical care – Job – HOPE!!!

Your name will grace many businesses and anyone who scorns at the lepers will answer to you. Who am I to judge. I am a leper.

? Six eyes = eyes 2 + sunglasses 2 + bifocals 2

I chased every devil
I was ill prepared
I have faith

I have strength
I am saved

That's the way uh huh, uh huh. I like it uh huh, uh huh

144,000 songs
Man, where is Brian Wilson when you need him

Lord help me
Give me the sales pitch
I need to convince:
drug companies /alcohol /tobacco/
government/Caesar

The system can be tweaked and everyone can live a better life. Give unto Caesar, what is Caesars and give unto the Lord what is the Lord's.

I have cast my net to the point the Lord is blocking me. I will cast no further, I will be content with whatever he gives me. For I know I have truly given it my all, without crossing the line of sanity.

Dear (2nd Wife),

I am not the Cook
I am not the Maid
I am not the Landscaper
I am spending time with our Father
I am sorry that disturbs you
I love you, bear with me
Nathan

I am sorry for calling you bitter. The devil has jumped on you.
A Godly woman
I pray GOD
Please remove the scales on her eyes – I cannot turn the light on to her heart

Performance – Do you want your GOD to dance? – Jerry Maguire
or will you dance for your GOD and Creator

Maybe I am the Lone Wolf McQuaid?
Because I am tired of teaching and not being heard – Seclusion – but I love people and I want to share

I refuse to roll up in a ball – Yo Adrian

Am I going to serve time, for spending time with our Father?

Stop dragging/Dragon me off course Devil, I want to go to Leper Land

Why can't a parent be a friend? What is it we are hiding? Does the devil have a secret?
I bet he does. Gootchy Goo
Secrets will rob you.

I hope the Terminator doesn't get me. Is he the boogie man we have heard so much about?

TRUST – Deception – Humiliation – Media – Drugs
The devil's mission statement:
DEATH

Nathan the Prophet
Wonderful Counselor
Servant of GOD
“A Godly Man”

I will once again, write a check for all that I have for your people.

Hey Deeds, can you use $1 billion?
Sure, why not – Mr. Deeds

The hole that I dig, becomes deeper and deeper. I hope it turns out like Shawshank Redemption. The Latter part of course.

Waz Up T. D.

I heard you

888 or 800 – I am not answering that one – that's a bill collector

Okay I get it
You want me to start writing again

The cruise ships will unload and reload giving everyone who seeks it, the Good News

I get it now – Bill Murray Scrooged

People from near and far will come
Listen – Field of Dreams
It will shock them
I know the truth, can we do anything about it?

I confess, the legal ways of our society and culture don't work for me.

I have a get out of jail free card. Do you have one Jack? – Clear and Present Danger

Oh well, I didn't think about that. I just wanted to serve our Father.

Act appropriately before our Father and you will be a Pro in his eyes.

We need housing for employees/lepers of Leper Land

Buy all Martyn Woods For cruise raffle

Porpoise – bottle nosed dolphin – Purpose

The first thing GOD showed me
GOD's beauty – man's existence
This is our LEGACY, embrace the lepers. We are people just like you.
You discriminate, he does not – KNOT

Book title
"If I were" Nathan the Prophet – Wonderful Counselor – Servant of GOD

"If I were" a Murderer
Thanks O.J.

Wait til you see the movie, your kids are going to love it – Marty Back to the Future

Something has got to be done about your kids – Doc

Your children need for you to be a parent and occasionally, they need a doctor.

You are resting me for being a servant of the Lord. Why can't I be forgiven for my mistakes? Are you crabs in a bucket? Ask Ralph.

80/20

Can you overlook the 20 and be content with the 80
Multi-lesson – stay with me now

Fed 15%
State 5%
GOD 10%
Can you live with 70%? X________

Peace and Love 100%

Your Temple will be filled with Bling Bling – Technology
So when you demonstrate your powerful hand, only the treasures of this world are lost and human life is spared and your temple can easily be rebuilt by the people of this World.

Your Earthly Entity, GOD's LEGACY TRUST LLC will be built in the same manner the Great Pyramids were built. With the life long efforts of your people. Everyone is a brick in GOD's Entity. Some used and some not.

They are just like cats, they can be trained, but it requires a tremendous amount of patience. No one really owns a cat. No one really owns a human.

Look up the definition of patience – ask Brian

You are enough to hold public confessions of faith
Don't forget planes and airstrip
But a performance is not necessary
Show your pride with the sign, the sign of GOD.
Do not erect or worship the sign
Conceal it in your heart
Reveal it in your wave
Love your fellow brother, we are all looking for different cheese stations – Who Moved My Cheese
I hit the Mother Lode
Good News – I share – I am not greedy.

I have been given ADHD and I like. Now that I know what ADHD is. How dare us for suppressing the future prophets for the devils glory, because of ignorance and greed.

Ghost of Christmas Present opens his curtains – Scrooge

I am one of you. Our forefathers are speaking to me. I went through life in a drunken stupor – stupid lost child. I have Aletheia – learn – unforget - TRUTH. Beware of false teachings, getting kicked in the teeth sucks.

Take off your masks. Lie down in a bed of snakes. You will be bitten. It really hurts don't it? Know that your salvation relies on your perseverance to never take your eye off you're creator. GOD, the one and only, your choice, he is always with you. He loves you unconditionally. Regardless.

I am becoming what I am meant to be.
Damn the torpedoes, I am coming in.

Ice has the lead. Okay you guys, I'm coming in.- Top Gun
The arrogant, vocally robust are responsible for the demise of the Knights Templar and Jesus Christ.

That whole "I am" thing works in real good. It is in the script. Imagine that.

Use your imagination and dip into the pool of Bathsheba? Cleanse yourself for yourself, not for the approval of others. Vain – Pain

Experience the past, so that you can articulate it. They have a purpose too. We are still paying a debt. What is the balance? Check please.
I had to become a commercial real estate investor to have the vision of your Temple.

Is the Indian in the commercial still crying over man's existence and harm done to our environment?

We have lived in Solomon's World long enough. Let us dwell in your World Lord. This one will do just fine. Just tweak it a bit. You've GOD mail.

Six dollar bill
The metric system may be easier, but I never got it.
I don't get it – Big
GRUMPS – Star Trek
Scary Revelation

Okay, I am starting to feel good GOD. Give them to me

Separate Leper Camps

How low can you go
Can you go to Da Flo
But Nobody Know
But You and
GOD

Poppies will make them sleep – Wizard of Oz
Ask your forefathers
There is no place like home – Immigration

Have you seen my home?

screw You, screw You, screw You
Who's next – Coming to America

Good Ship – Good Crew
Hoo Ray for ME
And screw YOU – Dad
Play it close to your vest and have a backup plan.

Rocky Marciano was how old when he beat Joe Lewis's ass? How old is your GOD? Can he be our Rocky? Because it sure has been Rocky and Rolly so far.

Okay okay, I like the place, but these damn bugs are eating my ass up. I'll wait in the car.

Don't waste your time on me, you are already the voice inside my head.
Come – Learn – Leave – Spread – You're holding up the line
Shit or get off the pot – Nathan

Be prepared to leave the bad lands most hurriedly. Age is a factor here. Wait till they really need The boogie man. Be trained to spot him, ADHD. Help him, he is a future prophet wanna be.
Some make it, some don't. But how do you know before you try. Are you willing to bet the family farm?

Go ahead, try to draw the sword. If it is not you, have a backup plan and live a wonderful life. Some will enjoy what they do. Some will strive for more. Cursed is the man that holds judgment over the starters and lagers. We need each other. There is plenty of shit I don't want to do. But to the person who is striving for more while picking up my shit, I pay you the respect that you deserve. Just a little bit is all I need, I have a plan and a backup plan. So watch out Devil. I am coming to get YOU.

Murdock, I'm coming to get you – Rambo II

I guess dipping in the ocean and lake was theatrics on my part. It is too damn cold to get wet. Is this the line of judgment we must all use. The code didn't work and the machine did break down.
Exercise good sense
The nuts are the ones that must perform
You, our GOD knows who you are
He always knows – A Christmas Story

We should have stuck up for him, it was not his blame – Shame to carry

We're suppose to stick up for the weak. We're suppose to stick up for Willie- A Few Good Men

I'll never know how much it Cost
To see my sin upon that Cross
I'm giving it all to you

Man this shit is so good, I think I'll buy my own tape-- TD Jakes

Answer: All in your Heart
Not in your pocket book. Give til it's comfortable. Put it in GOD's hands

Sorry, I can't pick up hitchhikers to Foley. You might be the devil.

I wouldn't have minded so much, but your slobbering dog would soil my interior.

Excuses are like assholes, we all got one – Platoon

Use them wisely

Hot Tub Time:
My fingers hurt – Nathan

Isn't the ocean beautiful?

I keep ending up at Point Clear, not Point Clear Alabama. Point Clear?
Probably not, it isn't for me either. Try this:
Let there be no misunderstanding
I AM is the Father
Jesus is the Son
Nathan is the Humble Servant

The Holy Spirit is all of this shit floating around us keeping score with consequences.

I see my footprints in the sand, I am is still carrying the load.
Try this:
Ban nothing, we need Judas
But if you want a check from GOD
You must be Clean

Quarterly drug test
Healed because it was detected
Don't suppress GOD's gifts to heal the nations any longer

Don't forget us misfit toys, we want homes too.
Boo-hoo Boo-hoo not another Christmas
Nobody wants us

Well you thought you were better than everyone else and you kept secrets. How can we TRUST you? What have you been waiting for? My 10 acres and a mule ain't showed up yet – DD

Answer: they ain't going to show up. Where did you lose your faith?

I ruined you by making you boss. Everyone is not supposed to be boss, it is their decision.

I need a physical exam. I hate smoke, leave that woman to GOD, hurts my lungs, but I like it up until I am done.

For ME – Ricky Bobby

Not the Planet of the Apes

How silly we are to laugh at other cultures because of our own ignorance – Borat

Cancel the party
Tell them I don't feel good
I don't give a shit
I am Hobnobbing
With the Almighty
I'll bring a note
This is beginning to look Eerie
I will check in Monday
But I will not be silenced, 911
That was easy
I have taken the path of least resistance my whole life.
One more round – Rocky V

Never give up
Help is on the way
Am I the help?

Are you the coconut that will pay full price Nathan? If you are, I didn't want to miss you. Car business.

What is a fair price? Tell us, don't make us barter in the street. We want to support you without getting screwed. Tell us what is fair and we will pay it.

Lost books of Nathan
Good news, I just found it – ask Brian

A. R. K.
Acts of Random Kindness – Evan Almighty
I can dig it. Who goes first Nathan?

Mr. Mom – the job sucks
and needs nourishment and appreciation
Your Spouse is an extension of you.

Step up – be a man in what ever capacity

Women respect your Men

We are an extension of each other

WILL > TRUST > GOD

What can I say, it is his patent – Nathan

What's up in Leper Land today – Cool Breeze – Doc Holiday

I need a holiday
If we took a holiday, could we have some time to spend together – Madonna

Can you handle this Jerry?
Sure Rick > File 13

Don't become too big, you will have no rest.
Make your judges accountable, you allow the Dragon to pierce my body, but not my heart and soul? Nathan

Hey, I am just working with the tools you gave me.

What was the name of that movie that was the counterpart to X-Men? All of the heroes had bizarre talents. Pee-Wee was the fart man. I guess with my gift Aletheia, I am able to articulate life's experiences through my own life experiences, as well as through the eyes of our forefathers via movie clips teaching us right from wrong.

Thank you Father – what a wonderful gift it is
your humble servant Nathan

Fishing – Hunt for Red October

Youth > TRUST > Mentor

How could you know?
I didn't even know. - Vinnie Barbarino

I like the fasting thing, but I am getting kind of hungry – Nathan

Whoops, I am not supposed to let the cat out of the bag. – Bulimia

Jolly Roger – Buddy
Shattered dreams hurt
If you bet the farm
Have a backup plan
Are you willing to lose all that you are because you are convinced you have the answer?
"GO FOR IT"
If not, sit down and shut up. I can't hear the real movers and shakers, don't be scared and don't leave me hanging.

No no, these are important, these are papers, not Gook Shit – Platoon

After You – you are a true friend

How big of a boat can you Captain, Gene?
Training

Sample it all, find out what you like. Strive for it. Your GOD wants you to have an abundant life. You do know your GOD wants that don't you? Have a plan for your goals, learn from my mistakes and the mistakes of your forefathers – Nathan

666
Don't look for signs
You are being tempted and giving in to temptation.

Why don't you just come on down? King of the Jews Ha Ha Ha

I need no visual miracle, but I pray you reveal your plan and all of my efforts will pay off.

Let me publicly confess your undying love to all of your people.
Your deeds will carry more weight than your words. Heal us Lord – Nathan

Sorry to be such an argumentative #$%&, but I have a list of questions that make you go Hmmmm...-- Nathan

It is not for you to know. Even my son Jesus didn't know the hour of your Savior.

I hate cliffhangers. Does this one turn out good? – Nathan

For all that TRUST in the Lord

I went blank – Nathan

Do you hear their cries for help? After their busted, be active for GOD
Drug Companies
Right Track, Wrong Tools
Didn't GOD give us 12 fruit bearing plants to heal the nations? Yes, I know I read that somewhere.

Where is the compass? Find it – Band of the Hand
I don't want to eat an alley cat. Care for animals as they care for you

Don't lose sight
Your father loves you more than any animal. Be aware. How hungry are you with the treasures of this world. That animals should needlessly sacrifice their skin off their back literally, so you can impress. How sad.
Image – Dances with Wolves

Dead carcasses rotting, what say you?

Is it that damn cold? – Nathan

I'm not taking a test
You take the damn test
Here are my notes.
Screw you – Nathan
Oh GOD – George Burns

This is real fun and I am laughing my ass off, but most of the shit is serious.

How can I count on my brother to do his part?

We're going to Leper Land till you get it.

Will I have to keep swearing after I am found out?
Yes, dammit George – Marty Back to the Future

You tell me people, which Nathan do you want?

Something for everyone – Bourbon Street

It's me – it's me – it's Earnest T.

You can come in
You can come out
M*A*S*H – Frank Burns lock up

Who is the nut?
Depends on the spin – O'Reilly

Wife called 4:04, guess I will submit, put on my game face and probably get drunk on wine. I deserve it. Oh shit! I can't get drunk, you might come tonight. I'll pace myself – Moderation.

You are the only one I can talk to Lord. Not even my Godly wife. Find forgiveness in me Lord. The devil is very powerful. Let me give them your new tool Lord. That will be in your favor and honor.

Let me just stop you from saying something you will regret later wife – You've got Mail

I would feel bad for showing my ass if she has planned a early surprise birthday party. If not, it's okay. I shouldn't show my ass anyway.

I don't give a#$%&
They are here for free food and drink and to lap up to you for donations – Back-to-School Rodney Dangerfield

Oh hell no, I'm not taking that, oh yes you are, Mama needs a nap.- Children's Motrin

How was your day dear?
Oh just another day of carrying the sins of the world on my shoulders kind of day.
How about you?

Please forgive me Lord, my forgetfulness has cost us another thought. My antennas are up.

But they are damaged, forgive me Lord for my sins.

Is this what people with Alzheimer's feel like. I don't like it. I want to go home, where it is safe.

Please fix my home.

I will deny you tonight, under protest, forgive me Lord. I love my wife.

Forgive me Lord. I will not deny you again. I know three times damn. Although my hand is sore, my heart soars. I respectfully request Coco – or heir and Holy Terror or heir. Coco – Chocolate Lab – Companion - Loyal, Holy Terror - solid white German Shepard – Bodyguard – Sight Dog.

Will you gouge out my eyes Lord?
I say I have suffered long enough, Father I have had enough strict discipline.

Andrew we won't except 2nd Pl. – Breakfast Club

We do not train to be merciful here,
Mercy is for the weak – Karate Kid

No discipline Johnny
Is this the Johnny I've heard so much about?
Give me some Johnny jokes baby.
Here's Johnny – Shining

Where do you lose it? Where is the line? What would you do with no lifeline? Call GOD

I must be conscious of every decision I make for fear of repercussions. I played drums hmmm...
Party On Wayne – Party On Garth

SIT YOUR MONKEY ASS DOWN!!!
Let us smoke awhile -Dances with Wolves
Deep Thought – Decisions - Future

I do not rely on people to sustain me. Therefore I speak my mind. Sorry if I offend you. But you know I am right. Please don't take me yet Lord.

O Tay I got sumptin to say --Buckwheat

If you thought you were the person that TD Jakes is looking for, considering you don't work there, how could you get to see the Wizard? I know in my heart. He is not behind curtains.

How long will you allow the devil to suppress my tongue?
I hate to put GOD on a deadline, but I am checking in on Monday, November 12, 2007. The devil drove me to drink. He is driving me crazy. I hope the medication will help get rid of him. Rather than sedate my Christianity and build my tolerance.

Why do we lie to our doctor? Secrets
Mafibachev – damaged, but delivered

How can I fix it, if I don't know what is broken. – Heartbreak Ridge

The truth shall set you freedom – Braveheart

Once I am discovered, I will no longer be able to move about you, to find out who you really are. The Mask will come off. The freaks come out at night. Heh heh

People are truly like cats, they require patience, they have tremendous tenacity. And even when we think we own them, they refuse to be owned. – Slavery

I hate the dating process, to find a mate with our masks on. Who are we? What are our motives? Are you as trapped as I am? How can you plan your escape and escape to where?

Can you go home?

Fortunately for me, I was born in a loving home. I can come and go as I please. I have rights as long as they don't offend anyone. When did the Lord's words begin to offend you? Did you do a self-examination to determine if the problem is within you? Take off your mask, it has blinders.

Girls Gone Wild – sorry dude, you offended the wicked and they framed you. Right to free speech or not, you're screwed.

Secrets weave a web. Too many secrets will trip you up during confrontation, especially if you are pandering for approval, votes or love.

I have the right answer. Follow me. You follow Drafiki, he know the way – Lion King

The answer is the Circle of Life. How will we leave Pride Rock? Plymouth Rock? Will our heirs be equipped with the teachings of Jesus Christ or the Devil?

Will our generation continue to do nothing to replenish what we have consumed, except procreate new consumers? What will our generation leave the World? At the present time, it looks like a big fat Debt.

Remember, remember. Go to the rulebook – Bible
All of the answers are written down.

But the rulebook is too damn long. Do you have it on CD? Yes. Well can you keep me entertained. I guess I am so lazy. I want to learn by watching a movie or playing a game. Although, you'll play hell getting anyone to play.

Who will lead us Lord?
I cannot
I am a drunk
I am a addict
I am a sexaholic
I am impatient
I have lost my tolerance
I am tired of working a flawed system

But I still have a DREAM!!!

If this prophet thing is my new gig, I can dig it. I need someone to take better shorthand that I.

Make sure everything is accurate, so you can use my words against me. I screw up – I am human.

If I didn't make any mistakes, how would I know if it is right?

Grow from Love – First Wives Club
How can I grow, when you're screwing my husband you deceptive bitch.

I know who I am
I know my purpose
I am Nathan the Prophet - Wonderful Counselor – Servant of GOD
Can you dig it?
Ha Ha Ha
Go home nut

Run Home Jack – Hook

Mission statement

Rectify all inhumanities man places on himself with the word of The Lord GOD Almighty!!!

KISS
Keep It Simple Stupid

Rock the boat, don't rock the boat baby, don't tip the boat over.

ALWAYS RESPECTFULLY QUESTION AUTHORITY

If they Look like shit
Smell like shit
Walk like shit
Talk like shit
They're probably full of shit or a duck.

Life and the money game

Age	
25 – 34	First quarter
35 – 44	Second quarter
45-- 54	Third quarter
55 – 65	Fourth quarter

Game Over or Over Time?

Where are you? Question: If you were to become disabled, how would you pay your bills? Better start preparing your Financial Ark while you have a strong back and spirit.

When will we make time for you my father? Your creation is beautiful and that is a genuine compliment, not meant to bloviate your ego. My excitement for my reward has diminished by the pain I am in enduring.

How to Win friends and influence people versus how to screw your friends and have them like you for it. You decide.

How many prophets have been silenced by our own ignorance? Were they burned at the stake?

I want to be Sniff
I want to be Scurry
Sorry, I am not an animal. Deal with the hand you have been dealt. It will work. I am convinced.
I want to be HIM – WWJ D.
I want to be Ha – Naysayers
Who moved my cheese?
GOD, I crave your cheese – Nathan

Lord, why show me these things and not allow me to change them. Are these the things that must happen or can happen.--Scrooge

Give us a Scooby Doo ending – Wayne's World

Would the book sell better titled:
Nathan the prophet, the Messiah, the Savior, the One and Only, the Almighty, the One to tell you all is well in the World, Go Ask Oprah.

This is something I must articulate, because I will never experience it. He has made that point quite clear. Our Father who art in Heaven, Hallowed be thy name. Thy Kingdom come, thy Will be done. On Earth, as it is in Heaven.

Let the name of Moses be stricken from everything and replaced with the name Ramses – 10 Commandment's

The significance of removing the name of Moses, is the attempt to remove his memory from our hearts, minds and future generations/History. The Egyptians always thought of things generationally and how over time, anything can be erased from history. Our society keeps chipping away at our belief that we are “One Nation Under GOD”. How many more generations will it take, for us to be so politically correct that there is no room for GOD in our lives. Just as there was no room at the Inn for Jesus Christ, there will be no room in our hearts for GOD. Who is this GOD anyway? Didn't his name used to appear on the U.S. Currency that was debased to the point of Worthlessness and Extinction?

If the U. S. economy fails, it will be a direct reflection on Judea Christian Principles and Capitalism. The two are intimately intertwined. I just have to wonder what the schools will be teaching my Great Grandchildren when or if that happens. I have a vision of that, but I'd prefer not to share with the class on this one.

Sign, sign, everywhere a sign. Do this, don't that, can't you read the signs – dumb ass

Are the signs right?

Don't follow them and see where that gets you.

Your son verbally challenges what he hears on TV. Do you think he should be checked out? – my grandmother's inquiry to my parents

Her name escapes me, probably because my dad's brother robbed me out of my check – LEGACY.

If it is killing you, why do you continue? I got a secret.

When you find out who you are and your purpose for GOD, you are the only gauge to compare yourself with. Until then, emulate people you want to become.
WWJD – no, I never wore one. I thought it was hokey at the time

Homosexuality --
He might not be okay with it, that's on you. But I am okay with it – Nathan

Well I am glad to know that you are okay with it. You pompous ass – (Thing One)

I heard about water purification ridding the saline for potable water. You are probably on the wrong track and you need some stoned kid in a garage to figure it out. Bill Gates gave us Windows and made more money than GOD. Do you need some more names. That would bore my ass. I get the point. Do you? We better catch that kid before he sees the wrong doctor.

This is a letter to future prophets. Wow, is this my first prophesy?

Hey you, lazy procrastinator. Put down that pipe and listen. If you're going to go through life medicated. Then bring something to this world that can help your neighbor.

1. Write your ideas down
2. reread number one – thanks Mr. Miagi If done right, no can defense. Crane technique.
3. 30 hours on tape lost to the devil. Are these the lost tapes of Nathan? Ha Ha

Have a credible source easily accessible to you, I am working on this path for you to examine your work. A Think Tank.

4. If this is a pain in the ass for you. Shut up and get a job. Hit the pipe when you can relax and be with your Father.

I know I'm laughing my ass off too.

If I am made in your likeness, your a goofy bastard too. I love you GOD. Where have you been all my life? – Nathan your humble servant

I love where this is going, keep them coming
And the hits keep rolling in

Let's roll
Let's sample a little of the hearts of heroes. The man that sticks out to me is that football player that gave up all of his future for his country/people/family/GOD.

How easy it is for GOD to fall to the back of the line. Even for me. I'm sorry Lord. Help me keep you first in my heart, not always in my words. We got business to take care of and we're moving on up to that deluxe apartment in the sky-- the Jeffersons

You made me a poor reader. Was this your deal with the devil?

The devil goes up to Georgia. But if I lose the devil gets my soul. This is when you spoke to me Lord. I want my fiddle made of gold. You let the people decide. I'll take my blessings from the rabble – It's a Wonderful Life. I already have yours.

And I believe you keep your promises.

I have a picture of Ralph in my Bible. I have not paid any attention to it, but I knew it was there.
I just looked at it. His arms are outstretched. My first thought was, where to now? My second thought was, is this it? The lot is straight, the cars are cranked, this ought to do it. Where's all the people?

Ralph – are you ready?

Get ready, get ready, get ready – TD Jakes

How do I get a book deal? Somebody has got to think this shit is as funny as I do.

I do – failed commitments, please take off the mask.
10% in the bucket ought to do it. It worked for me, but what do I know, I'm a leper.

Man these cigarettes are killing me. You got to die of something, I guess. My son wants me to quit smoking, so he can spend more Quality time – ask Austin
The amount of time concealing my secret world, would have been better spent with him. The devil is robbing me.

Humans are not logical – Spock
Whoever said we were – Kirk

You don't own me – First Wives Club
Look at my mess, I need help.
Help – I need somebody – Beatles
Help, I've fallen and I can't get up.

I've always liked Stephen Wrights style of humor. Dry and sarcastic.

You know that feeling you get leaning back in your chair right before you lose your balance and bust your ass? I feel like that all the time – Steven Wright

I feel like I have fallen and can't get up – Nathan – Age

Honor your Mother and Father even when they're ignorant. My parents are far from ignorant concerning smarts. With GOD, I don't know. I have been ashamed to ask. Forgive me Lord. My past times don't make me the best Witness for you.

That one hurts

(Thing One) was the first to call me Holy Roller – I kind of liked it.

I am surely to be blind, because women are gorgeous in all shapes and sizes.

You know there is a GOD – Coming to America

Was the Shock GOD a Prophecy?

Because I am enjoying screwing with people and being the invisible Mario.

Dog, I feel your pain. Refer to Mrs. Doubtfire for your forgiveness. Are we really brothers from a different mother? I use the N. word all the time. Maybe it's time to turn a new leaf. Stop picking the fly shit out of the pepper. You are imprisoning your own people.

GOD doesn't like you. I don't like you. You are users of this system. Ask (Thing One), he loves to tell this story. How he gets over on his peers, so he can be first at the table. He is the one that should be last, if even invited.

This is the song that never ends, it goes on and on again my friend – Nathan

Your silly, no your silly. Are you having fun with this One Life the Lord has given you?

I am looking for signs – ask (2nd Wife)
I am headed to the pass
Had to write it down before GOD

I am not organizing all this shit, so you can forget it.

We can send it in as the babblings of Nathan. Read by the author – nope, I don't want that job either. An ADHD stupid screw.

Whitey/Stoney can you get my bag. Nathan's version movie with Hank – Jim Carrey – him carry
Someone please help me carry this CROSS.

No wonder GOD did not allow me to reach Wikipedia.

Is this the video game that alerted the bad guys – trailer park – Alex
The last shall be first, respect your brother
There were sure enough warnings even for my ADHD ass

You said my torment would get greater. It is true, like birthing pains. I must get this out. Number one: your plan or number two: the devils plan. I'll take curtain number one. dumb ass, jackass

Not a mistake of mine, but a mistake of culture

run home Jack
    Jack ass – Happy Gilmore Adam Sandler Movie
run home Jack ass
Good advice. How's it working out for you? He loves you. Forgive my damaged antennas.

I want one of those remotes
Click? First a boat, a loan again. Where do I start GOD?

That payment is going to eat you up – my first toy – 74 Corvette

While I am trying to sell.

Materialism is a whole chapter. A very long chapter. Let them play the game. It explains it better than I. I am tired again. I wrote the President again – predictable – Forrest Gump

Where is Lieut. Dan, Gene?

I've got money now. That's good. One less thing to worry about.

Worry will kill you faster on the inside – cancer? It will drive you insane. Don't worry, be happy. Our Father loves us. Enjoy now. You will be going home soon enough. Which house, it's up to you.

I don't have a clue what the Lord will have me write next, but I feel good. Da Na Na Na I knew that I would, so good – Nathan/Little Richard

Richie Valens flight
Pray that your plight is not in the winter – somewhere in the Bible

I am driving my brother, like Michael the Archangel. Plus I don't have to worry about going through detection devices. I need my medication. You Bastards – Braveheart

My image of living in the US as being the best place to be has been a little shaken. I am proud to be an American. But this sucks. Have we really defeated Long Shanks? I am tired of the scraps from his table. SEC? Security Exchange Commission

Okay is that what you call it now.

I want my SEC – Gator Growl – Go Gators – Smothers Brothers
The little Faggot got his own jet airplane
The little Faggot he's a millionaire

You have got to be kidding Yo Yo tricks for my drunk ass.
Taste Great!!! Less Filling!!!

I admire you for sticking it out. But you suck, for this stage environment.

Lord help me reveal that you can be all things to all people

Let me close the greatest Sale of my life

World's Greatest Salesman
That is what we really are. The devil has many tools in his bags. We all are distracted and attracted to see whats inside. Don't give up Santa Claus. I like him. Teach your children about their check – they will receive on their 18th birthday – Nathan. Sorry kids, compounded interest needs time to mature.

Use judgment please, of course take care of the orphans. That is where you will find him and you are not quite ready – Maturity

I am trying not to sin like my forefathers did. I don't want to wait 40 years, if I can even make it that long – Nathan

I want an Umpa Loompa now Daddy – Willy Wonka

But that girl has a fine ass. Girl, you lookin so good, somebody ought to sop you up with a biscuit – Coming to America

Cover-up Nikki, you never know when there are N's around – Band of the Hand

Nikki – ask Prince or whatever sign he is

My guess is less is more, but not with clothing

You don't have to be a stick in the mud though

Don't let the latest fashions drive you $$$
Just cover your ass

I wrote a book about myself. I know everything in it, but I don't have a freaking clue what is in it. I have five original tapes in a sealed federal express package mailed to my parents. Can I start the bidding at $1 million for GOD's LEGACY TRUST LLC.

I wish I had $1 million – It's a Wonderful Life

This money is for you GOD. This buds for me. Your grace is enough for me. The things of this world, given to us by you. All natural?
This is a pain in the ass, but it requires more labor. The lepers are coming, the lepers are coming – ask the Tinman
They are from the school of knowledge – they know what it is to really eat an alley cat. Third world impoverished countries suck. Let's fix this. As the beacon country, One Nation under GOD.
They really "Will Work for Food", not entitlement.

I am looking at a fat ass (Yeah I checked it out., I'm only human) white girl with a black baby. Where is that babies daddy?

If you love them, okay. Interracial marriage – but make sure you read all of the ingredients on the back.

What is black and white and red all over? – a newspaper

Forget the color, know your mate.
Can they be made accountable? Not by your power, don't even try. Only through Jesus Christ can you understand the Father.

Let's do something different. Let's go to church. Maybe they were just fixing to call me or maybe they are still waiting.

I am waiting for the National Enquirer to come put this angel out of my misery.

We have no homosexuality in our country. Ha Ha Ha Iranian Leader
Our ignorance – they are in complete control – control freak – let them decide – let GOD judge – step back nonbelievers.

All we are saying
is give peace a chance – Billy Jack

If you don't know how hard it is to be heard, you are probably dead. Another one bites the dust and another one gone and another one gone, another one bites the dust. Heh Heh

If you are looking for the devil. He is on the front row.

I must be on the front row – commercial

I wouldn't mind a N like Colin Powell for a Father in law. Overcome racism. It's hard to get all your people to overcome ignorance. Then we can identify the N's from the rest of the colors – and heal them. What color was N anyway? shimmer 666 felt

If I can change. And you can change. We can all CHANGE!!!
 - Rocky IV

Answer mailbox
had you going there didn't I. You lucky devil – skunk

Who do you think is the devil?
My name is nobody – Henry Fonda

My mom is first to call, one o'clock one hour grace period, from high noon

Mom, I didn't know it, but I am a writer.

But you hate to read.
Yeah, but I did what I had to do to reinvent myself. To pick myself up from the mire. Somewhere along the way, I met GOD. And we are going to see the Wizard. If it is the last thing I ever do. Auntie Em is sick and needs GOD to heal her.

I didn't know I was supposed to be looking for a prophet. If a prophet crawled out of your ass would you know one. Prophet Nathan you dumb ass.

Here's a sign
I sat in front of a boat named Promised Land II no shit. And a humbled man says, I can only dream to rent one.

Ask of your Father, you shall receive.

I am a coon ass
Not a dumb ass
I am a dumb ass with ADHD

Coon ass with my senses

Crazy like a fox
What did a coon ever do to you?

Momma used to just scare them off with a broom – Forrest Gump

N joke, do tell – Wild Hogs

First Dr. – I can take off that leg in 15 seconds
Second Dr. – I can take off that leg in 10 seconds
Third Dr. – that ain't shit, I can take that leg off in 8 seconds

Mame that Coon. (Name that Tune)

Public Schools
try this maze
in > ========= out

Can the system be dumb-ed down any further? I remember listening to a talk show and this very smart young lady from Calif. had married a man from Virginia. Somehow their intellect was gauged and the woman realized that her husband had gained more knowledge than her, while scoring substantially lower in grades through their respective school systems.

All of this soldiering/learning is bull shit – Heartbreak Ridge

Hey, is watching chicks ass a class? it sure is. The technique can be a real problem. – Rape – Pedophile – Incest – SHITHEAD College

WWJD
The Wonderful Counselor can pass the buck

You can reach me on the Bat phone, but don't bother me unless it's important.
I'm enjoying the second half of my life. Scooby Doo

A lot of doctors are us ADD goofy folks. We don't have time for petty things like paying bills. We're too busy trying to heal the world. - Dr. Nathan

I hereby award, by the power vested in me, by the Wonderful Land of Oz – U.S.- Knowledge/Truth

To you Lion – Courage and Knowledge

To you Tinman – Compassion and Knowledge

To you Scarecrow-- well, you already have been given knowledge, so you can have all of the rest of the shit the others have.

Dorothy – What have you learned?

If I told you, you would laugh. So I'll let the scarecrow tell you.
You're screwing up – Nathan

Hey, this whole cussing thing has got to stop.

Dammit George, not yet. – Back to the Future

Adm. I've noticed your use of colorful metaphors since we have been on this planet?-- Spock

It is the only language this culture understands if you want to be heard – Kirk
Star Trek IV

They Ignant
Do you understand Ignant – ask a Louisianian

I met a man walking up from the beach with all the fishing gear, he says he forgot his bait. What bait shop do I use? I like the discrimination idea, that always stirs up the N's and they stir up the Honkeys/Donkeys.
And somebody gets paid.
"Shake Down"

Let's follow the money/memory trail
Give them a get out of jail free card and watch them work your magic.

I am at the beach. I just had an epiphany. Maybe I will be able to see GOD do his work. My big head is blind and my stiff drunk head has no conscious.

Sex before marriage, I concede you are right. Ask Amy and Andrew or is it Jack and Jill?

Jack fell down and broke his crown, Jill came tumbling after

The man is the head, take your place.

Not here, in the ring. You only fight in the ring, Tommy Gunn. – Rocky V
Devil, this is the ring you've been wanting – Media

We all thought you wanted a diamond ring. Brought to you by De beers-Commercialism – Materialism

Lord, are you pissed?

Chill a little – my fingers hurt

Have you ever seen the shimmering of the sea?

I love the water, it is a wonderful gift.

I cannot reproduce the thoughts. They are from you Lord. Do not allow my tracks to be covered. I've carried the worry of the world long enough – Mercy – Uncle Nate

Sorry Shauna, for not being a part of your life. I can't wait to hear if you have the shining.

Past a leper on the way to the men's room. He was disgusting, perfect for the movie.
I said, how's it going?
3 seconds pass
It's going well.

Fine, we are just fine. The lie of the devil – ask David Walker

To think I actually thought this leper might rob me and take my wallet. I only have a dollar. Perfect for the script. Hey, I guess we now know what happened to the other mother freaking dollar. Riddle: three men check into a hotel.

Answer: Nathan GOD it.

I'll try Lord, but I will challenge you on the blame game. You made the serpent.
Grace, Ahh it feels so good.
Plead your case you pole smokers and bush biters. He loves you. Arthur, the Bach Family will always Endure and we will Endure this. But know this, your kids could be future prophets.

Where are my accusers? Where are the ones I have touched?

Will they speak for me or deny me?

It's looking real good or crash and burn – Maverick

If we infringe on the rights of the movie companies
screw 'em
It's coming anyway
Who heads up the Supreme Court anyway?
Let him tell us there is no Santa Claus. – Miracle on 34th St.

Birth of the Leper Party.
Let's see, who do I pick, Nathan?
I've always liked newt1162.

Yeah, but that was your porn handle good buddy.
You asked.

What about his vice? I don't have a clue, let him decide. But I already know I like his wife. She will do great things.

I can see it in her – Braveheart

Come on baby light my fire

Good news, I found them. I got them right here.
Look harder – Lion King

This is the living Word of GOD with animation. I had been here the whole time. Let's connect with every tribe, every nation. Lets freaking do it.

We keep saying it "Let's Roll"

I love that commercial of a room full of do nothings. Pick it up, right Bill?
Somebody has to have the vision and pick it up, so that we all may have direction. What direction is our world heading in right now? as we speak? It's pretty frightening.

These are science fiction stories about the second coming of the Lord. Dammit George, you have to cuss or they won't hear you.

Okay, it will be a great freaking movie. Wait about bringing the kids Rated PG XIII.

All of my shit can go on eBay for sale. This should start GOD's LEGACY TRUST LLC. Deal?

The devil got all my mail.
I hope the one with the loudest trumpet got my e-mail – Oprah

Can you hear me
It's okay, we're safe now

Come out, Come out, Wherever you are. Warriors, come out and playyyyyy – Warriors

Greed-Draggin
Cultural Diversification – Blood Sport – Roger Moore thief, air balloon, can't lift treasure

Leo it's okay, you can go home to your family – Lionheart

Children, I have candy and sweets and it is all free today. S/Chitty Chitty Bang Bang
Say shoe city as fast as you can, over and over again. A new song combo sample.

Can you supersize me for $.39. He loves you. He wants to heal you. Hey, I like it. A GOD tax. Let them pay until it's comfortable.
You healed my baby, thank you Lord Jesus Christ. Thanks are necessary, can you pass that bucket. No not that one. GOD's bucket.

I kind of wanted to go home, but you're not done. It is 3:28 is five o'clock okay?

You are home. Don't you love it. Watch the Purple Martyns.

Why are you coming home half drunk?

I ran out of money. Shit, get off my ass. I am spending time with our father. Who's Yo Daddy.

Is the Harley Davidson doing it for you? You missed your chance Terry. I'll bet you will work your skinny little, floor flushing ass off now, won't you? Tell me, will you serve me? How much do you need?

I guess we don't have to reinvent the wheel after all. The lepers will fulfill all of your needs. Costa Rica sounds great, but how about Prichard Alabama. How about N. O. not no, but Hale N. O. Dem sum crazy fukas ober der.

My wife bought dinner for the family on vacation from serving the renovation needs in New Orleans. A dinner seemed the least she could do for the fearless warriors that forge into harms way. Armed only with the Bible, Faith and Love for other human beings.

Give me the tools of the devil. They work pretty good GOD. Are you hearing me my Father? Can you tell I am scared shitless?

His word gives me comfort. I will hear sounds of war and wars to come. These things must come.

Is must a scroll down option?

Yes, I would like to see everything on the menu.

Do you want the buffet, the whole Enchilada, the whole ball of wax?

Well, you got your work cut out for you don't you? --NEWT '08

Oh man, he is a Republican. No, I am a leper and I am sick and I leave among you.

You know GOD knows his shit. When he makes me mess up words like live. It truly is the living word.

It will take centuries, hopefully, to dissect all of this shit.

Hopeful Prophecy

How 'bout it monkey
Are you ready to Tango or Rumble?

Be afraid. Be very afraid.

The signs are off the chart.

We have seen what man could do. Holy shit, did you have any idea Batman?

Iraq – Freedom

But what about the bullies?
Do what you got to do. I got your check and your medicine.

How are your children, by the way?
Good, you call U. S. if you got a problem. Other than that, I'm ready to take my monkey ass to the house.

Forgive me Lord, for I have sinned. I role-played immoral sex and we laughed.
Devil screws the Lamb. Ha Ha Ha
Isn't that what's happening every day in our lives?

You are a sly old fox GOD. It makes for a great script.

It was not I who was sleeping, but my brother – Platoon

Excuses, Excuses –WAKE UP – I Am Coming...

I am aware of the serpent now. I will put my foot upon the head of the scorpion. And splat. No more problem. This is for you Zodiacs @#$%&'s

Sorry for the sin, can you have the Martyns come and take care of the pests/devil?

Draggin / Dying
their / your tongue

Jackass

Okay, how do I contact Time Warner Books? Is the owner a devil? – Ted Turner
Maybe Jane Fonda wants some salvation? Surely her father did. Ask him, he is a nobody – My name is Nobody

Are you embarrassed to ask our forefather questions? I don't blame you. In every environment I speak of GOD. They want to stone me, so I did it for them.

Ahh, the tree of life
Frick you and your little dog too.

Futuristic stories, you are a riot.

You can call me Joe. I helped Nathan. Joe Fox, just Joe – You've Got Mail

All y'all can have the peace prize, I want that GOD Reward.
Catch Lucky, he's got Lucky Charm's. They're magically delicious. It wasn't gold, you jackass. It was medicine and food.

Am I Doinking you yet? Pay attention Stoney – I Love Ya

Who will be the first to present their idea before the Lord? The Lord will grant you your patent. Thank you for sharing.

You can plead your case to the court most high.

I am selling.
I like both my heads, even though one is badly beaten. It is time to masturbate or are you the apprentice baitor? Let's go fishing, I'll tell you all about it.
Thanks Dad – Boys
Thanks Mom-- Girls

Whatever, you gauge your child's faith and direction. Step up and be Parents.

Who will fill in my pieces Lord? Will you come again or is this time for keeps?

Smoke the day's last cigarette, trying to make it through

I'm avoiding conversation, but Father, I Love people too

Don't let me die with a broken heart Lord. Your people do not know where to turn.

Show them the TRUTH, Oh GOD

We are hungry. We are ripe. Don't let me be the sacrifice. I still have my marbles, they've been freeze-dried like Buck Rogers or is it Roger that?

Dew Circuit
Break Out
We are the Dew, move over.
Let U. S. Dew what we Dew Best
SAVE

Can you afford not to be in good hands? – GOD

Sprint ahead. I am in an epic tale, if I rescue Zelda. Can I win?

Wife asked me to go to parents. Audubon here I come.

You just can't keep those Bailey's down – It's a Wonderful Life

I'm a Bailey on my Mother's side.

LETTER TO:

(2nd Wife)

November 10, 2007
(2nd Wife),

I am terribly remorseful for not controlling my tongue.

I told you that I was not well and to cancel the party.

What did you expect?

I am sorry that my tolerance level is at zero.

But I would be remiss if I didn't point out to you my observations concerning your Christianity.

Your girlfriend (Thing One)s wife (Thing Two), Hit on me all night long.

Did I stop the party and make an announcement that although (Thing Two) knew that not only am I a heterosexual, but also married to the wonderful woman across the room hosting the party.

The only thing he was focused on was the serpent between his legs. So I felt that if this is the way homosexuals conduct themselves, I shouldn't have any problem calling a spade a spade to their face.

Or in this case, putting a mirror to their face and asking, you either suck Dicks or you don't suck Dicks.

What concerns me is that a Godly woman such as yourself, will hold herself accountable sexually, as well as her partner, yet allow the epitome of sin to slither in the front door. Check out Revelations 2: 14-17

(2nd Wife), I love you!

But, which version of the Bible are you going to believe and follow?

Nathan

MANIC TRIP TO:

DALLAS, TEXAS

Manic Trip to Dallas

Where do I begin?
Just the facts please,
Just the facts.
It stings more.

After google searching a Small Christian Publishing Co. I noticed it was in Dallas. Perfect, I could drop off my book and buy cars in the Dallas Market and make a check. I needed that check, because in my mind I had been put out. After many wrong turns and asking help from one individual in the neighborhood, I found it. Mr. Kuran was not home. What to do now? Bishop T. D. Jakes is in Dallas, I'll just pay him a visit. As I was driving to Dallas it occurred to me that I did not have his address. What do I do? Call 911, after all I am crazy, right. I called 911 and a nice foreign man stayed on the line until I found a place that would be easy for the officers to find. Bought a pack of smokes, a diet coke and awaited their arrival.

When the officers arrived we were all being very cautious. I had them both read my letters. I asked them to take me to my ministers house because I had a mental disorder and would get lost. He assured me it would be no problem to find and wrote out the directions himself. I managed to only have a few missed turns and I finally found the Potters House. The gentleman allowed me through the gate and I parked. I stood outside my car a little cocky that I had something that T. D. wanted. I was soon met by three gorillas headed up by Capt King Kong. I knew I had an ass whipping coming if I didn't alter the situation at hand. I asked Capt King if I could personally deliver my package and was told T. D. was not in. He told me he could deliver the three years of my work to him personally. I don't think so. I'll give him a bribe. So I gave him the mental discrimination letter to give to T. D. I asked him to sign it, as well as the other two witnesses. They refused to sign something that was not a legal document. I went to my car and got something to write Capt Kings name on and gave him the letter. I never received help from T. D. so I can only assume that the Potters House is not in the SHAKE DOWN business and I was at the wrong house of the Lord for that. I apologized for my behavior, shook their hands and parted company. But my mission was still incomplete and I was tired of waiting. So I went back to the hotel room to rest and contemplate. What do I do now? I know, I'll call 911 again, they were helpful last time. MISTAKE!!! I told the operator that I was having a mental breakdown and needed to speak with my minister. I did not want an ambulance or police. She told me standard procedure was to send law enforcement. I told her I already had gone through that on the first 911 call. Please cross reference. She began asking more questions and I told her that I was through with her.

This is where it gets really cool. I kick back on the bed to wait for T. D. to come busting through the door. So I bought the movie that I had been wanting to see for awhile. Pirates of the Caribbean Last Episode. I soon realized that I was Jack Sparrow, but of course I have been the hero that saves the day in countless movies. But this time it seemed to completely fit because of my cultural diversity and the present mission at hand. The movie that I had wanted to produce, was already available thanks to our Father. Watch it again now with the pretense that Jack is the second coming of Jesus Christ and me Nathan the Prophet.

I did not get far into the movie before the police arrived. I looked through the peep hole and realized once again I was betrayed. I quickly thought I would not let them in and then realized they would just kick the door in and cause a big scene, which is what I was trying to avoid in the first place. As they entered my room, I was a courteous man revealing all of the secrets I had been hiding my whole life and had robbed me of having a full life with my dad and mom and entire family. Freedom, right? Wrong. The officers really didn't want to arrest me. My dumb ass insisted, hindsight being 20/20 a mental facility would have been a lot more pleasant. But the idea of one who flew over the cuckoo's nest resounded in my head and I didn't want any new Indian friend putting me out of my misery. I am sane. I just can't get anyone to listen.

I was booked, stripped to my underwear and stuck in a box. A very small box. What have you gotten yourself into this time Ollie? I decided to follow up with Capt. King and see if T. D. would come and get me. I was allowed out for my phone call and was instructed to the rack of phone books. My reading glasses were of course confiscated and I requested help from Palmer and K – something. They told me they would help in a minute. The common answer. A blonde lady passed by and I asked for her help and she smarted off to me and that was all it took for me to lose it. Feeling another ass whipping coming, I retreated to my cell. Once in my cell I screamed, all I wanted was help reaching my minister. The black woman gorilla snarled that my minister was T. D. I am sure she was thinking, don't you white folk have Billy Graham. So I proceeded to cause a disturbance by beating on the door. A new white Kong emerged and we exchanged words. I hope they are all of tape, because not only did he let me know he had a hard on for me, he would do all in his power to make me pay. Including extending my stay and he made a comment about not having sex with my wife for awhile. Now, I have no proof of this, but did the initial officers decide that my sexual perversions or needs should be shared with the class. I felt like they all shared a laugh at my expense. Completely ignorant to the symptoms and characteristics of a person with ADHD.

After I grew tired of beating on the door. I laid down to gain control of my senses so as not to lose it and slip into a state of mind I could not get back from. Afterwords, this white Kong delivered the number to the Potters House by slipping a post it note under the door. It was after hours by now and he said "here's the number to your minster". I posted the post it note in the window of my cell for all to see. I have that post it note. The jail has the video. They left me all night with nothing but my underwear and a Rambo outfit. I finally caved in to them and requested a mattress and blanket. They did get around to it finally. I was freezing and utilized the blanket as a tent and sat on the Rambo outfit to keep my ass and feet warm.

The next morning, I was brought breakfast. Two boxes of cereal, white milk and a sugar packet. I ate the sugar packet for strength, but I was either to hard headed or just not hungry to eat the cereal and I don't like whole milk.

I made repeated request to see a mental or medial doctor. I was told that I would be under observation. If I didn't have a firm grip on my sanity because of my relationship with GOD Almighty, I can see where a man with less mental capacities could definitely slip over the edge. I did start to experience claustrophobia and requested to get out. I was not out long before lunch was served and I decided to keep my strength and eat. I went back to my cell with the door open. I was half way through and I was full when a white gorilla came by and said we need to close the door. I told her that I was through and wanted to go back to the TV. She told me no, finish your lunch and closed the door. Finally a pretty African-American woman opened the door after my repeated knocks were ignored. Thank GOD for her. She must still be full and not bitter. Kojak on the other hand reminds me of the nut in the Green Mile. So Kojak, how many licks does it take to beat down a mental prisoner?

Through the help of my new found friend, I found that my

parents had been in Irving since 5:30 A.M. And started the bail process, so it was just a matter of time now. I engaged in a stimulating conversation with an intelligent black man that had experienced all the poisons available. He concurred that the really dangerous poison is the Elixir that caused Mary Jane to be suppressed in the first place. The weed was cutting into elixir sales. It was bad for business, so it must be bad and should be made illegal.

I am going to request that my lawyer, who I have not spoken to yet, sue the city of Irving, the State of Texas and the Federal Government for suppressing the medicine provided by my GOD to heal the nations. Rev 22: 1-3 and for the lack of training of mental illnesses by government officials. They have been trained like the gorilla guards from the Planet of the Apes.

Hear No Evil
Speak No Evil
Cause Evil to stay with us Indefinitely.

I do not want my Federal Government to take out another loan to give to me, but fund a new campaign to heal us all. This campaign is to raise money to put into GOD's LEGACY TRUST designed to fund research and crusade to feed the poor around the world and exchange medical ideas with cultures that continue to survive, even faced with the most difficult adversities. They must have found cures with natural plants and herbs. We need to tap their knowledge and not discount them like they are a bunch of savage Granny Clampetts. Secrets can be revealed if we are not fearful of the repercussions. Would I do it again. Of course. Will Stoney hiding in the closet come forward with his ideas. Highly Unlikely. What a shame we have suppressed the creativity of the Human Mind all to chase the Gold in Solomon's mine.

MY LAST WILL AND TESTAMENT

MY LAST WILL AND TESTAMENT

ASSETS
COLONIAL BANK ACCT# ******3693
ASSORTED REAL ESTATE ACCESSIBLE BY PUBLIC RECORD
99 HONDA ACCORD EX
PERSONAL BELONGINGS

LIFE INSURANCE
JACKSON NATIONAL LIFE INSURANCE
ACCT#______________________________
FACE VALUE $300,000.00

AT TIME OF MY DEATH:

JAMES AUSTIN ISBELL TO RECEIVE ALL ASSETS AND $50,000.00 FROM JNLI
(SSN XXX-XX-XXXX)

LAUREN ANTOINETTE ISBELL TO RECEIVE $50,000.00 FROM JNLI
(SSN XXX-XX-XXXX)

THE REMAINING INSURANCE MONEY IS TO HANDLE BURIAL ARRANGEMENTS, AND ALL OTHER LEGAL EXPENSES.

THE REMAINING JNLI DEATH BENEFIT IS TO BE USED TO ESTABLISH A LIMITED LIABILITY CORPORATION.

THE NAME OF THIS L.L.C. IS :
"FROM THE ESTATE OF NATHAN J. ISBELL"
"ENDEAVOR TO PERSEVERE"

THE NAME OF THIS L.L.C. IS TO BE PROMINENTLY DISPLAYED ON EVERY SEMI-ANNUAL DIVIDEND CHECK SENT TO HEIRS AND CHARITIES.

ALL ASSETS OF THIS L.L.C. ARE TO BE MANAGED BY EDWARD JONES. ACCOUNT NUMBER TO BE ESTABLISHED AT SAME TIME AS THE L.L.C.

L.L.C. IS TO RETAIN 50% OF THE YIELD, EDWARD JONES TO DISBURSE 50% TO
QUALIFIED MEMBERS AND CHARITIES

DISBURSE:

MEMBERS	90%
GOD LEGACY TRUST LLC	10%

RULES AND REGULATION FOR MEMBERS AND/OR CHARITABLE ORGANIZATIONS
****

*EACH QUALIFIED RECIPIENT IS ENTITLED TO AN EQUAL VARIABLE SHARE OF DISBURSEMENTS AT AGE 18.

*MUST REGISTER WITH INVESTMENT BROKER 30 DAYS PRIOR TO EACH BIRTHDAY WITH PROOF OF LINEAGE AND BIRTH CERTIFICATE

*NO LIENS MAY BE ATTACHED

*NO BACK PAYMENTS

*ORGANIZATIONS THAT FAIL TO REGISTER WITHIN 2 YEARS WILL BE DELETED AND PROCEEDS TO GO INTO QUALIFIED RECIPIENT FUNDS

*IF INVESTMENT BROKER FEES ARE EXCESSIVE OR THE RATE OF RETURN FALLS BELOW 10 % FOR 2 YEARS IN THE LAST 5 YEARS A MAJORITY VOTE OF QUALIFIED RECIPIENTS MAY CHANGE INVESTMENT BROKERS TO A DIFFERENT LEGITIMATE BROKER UNDER PRE-SET GUIDELINES. TIE NO CHANGE

*MINIMUM LEGACY CHECK IS $100 AFTER FEES AND EXPENSES, OTHERWISE ACCOUNT WILL RETAIN 100 % UNTIL THIS CAN OCCUR

*ONLY DIRECT BLOODLINE LINEAGE QUALIFIES, NO EXTENDED FAMILIES

*SPOUSE OF QUALIFIED RECIPIENTS DOES QUALIFY AS MY REPLACEMENT UPON MY DEATH

*MUST REGISTER ALL BIRTHS OF YOUR BLOODLINE WITHIN FIRST YEAR. INCOME STREAM MAY NOT BE SOLD FOR ONE LUMP SUM. BOTH OF THESE INFRACTIONS RISK LOSING YOUR SHARES AT A MAJORITY VOTE. TIE NO

*FUND MUST HAVE A POSITIVE YIELD OR THERE WILL BE NO DIVIDEND CHECK FOR THAT PERIOD
*IF NO HEIR, DIRECT PROCEEDS TO GODS LEGACY TRUST LLC

LETTER TO:

THE EDITOR

I have the answer that we all seek. How will we pay for Socialized Health Care?

"LEGACYWILLANDTRUST.COM"

I am in the process of building a website that will enable everyone to log in and create themselves a Living Will and TRUST FREE of charge. You will answer a series of questions just like I did when I created my own LEGACY on Legal Zoom. (Cost me $500.00 that I don't really have) Only my website will also have a special directives clause and this is where a new found taxable income is created. As I did in my own TRUST, I left my assets and a portion of my Life Ins benefits to my immediate loved ones. The rest of the Life Ins benefits, I have directed it to establish an LLC. This creates an entity that dividends can be channeled through to stockholders. In this case, the stockholders are all my future bloodline. They qualify as stockholders at age 18. They will receive a semi-annual dividend check from me via the Financial Planner of my choice prominently displaying "From the Estate of Nathan J. Isbell", "Endeavor to Persevere". The website will allow freedom on naming your LLC at your death. So you may pass along whatever words of wisdom you want to all of your future heirs for an eternity.

The new found taxable income will be used at the discretion of our Government. I can only hope for a reduced flat tax like the present Capital Gains tax of 15% and they use these funds to re-build Social Security.

Furthermore, during these series of questions that are used to determine your Last Will and Testament. There will be a series of questions on how you want your LEGACY to be split up amongst your heirs, charities, passions and GOD.

One very important question prior to all charities being listed is concerning:

GODS LEGACY TRUST LLC.

"GOD has only ever asked for 10% and will give it back to future generations ten fold.

What percent of your LEGACY would you like to leave to GOD and his people. _______%".

for more info "GODSLEGACYTRUST.COM".

I'm building this site as well. GODS LEGACY TRUST LLC will be the earthly entity that channels GODS Blessings to heal his people.

GODS LEGACY TRUST LLC
will re-invest 50% of its yield and disburse 50% for socialized healthcare.

We have all been wondering how to pay for health care. GOD has shown us the way. By investing in ourselves and our Creator.

Nathan J. Isbell
P. O. Box 1371
Gulf Shores, Al. 36547

If you decide to publish this, I would like to remain anonymous while I finish building my websites.

CC:
Atlanta News Journal
USA Today
NY Times
Washington Post
The Islander

THE FINAL CHAPTER

“IT'S THE FINAL COUNTDOWN”

September 5, 2009

This LEGACY Donated by ___________________

Funded by the people through GOD's LEGACY TRUST LLC.

Brian's legal quandary

The GOD Father has lots of buffers

Clip – "Show Me" – Christine

I knew he would do it, the ancestors doubted then jumped aboard – Mulan

Our lives are such a microcosm of time.

I am a humble servant of the Lord, all that I am and do are for his glory and praise.

David wanted to build a house of cedar to honor him. The prophet Nathan says "GO FOR IT" then has a discussion with GOD. GOD needs no house. He is an entity in our hearts, minds, bodies and souls and demands an earthly entity to glorify him for all that seek him. For all eternity.

I have been tempted by the devil. He is all around us and very powerful. I rebuke the devil, for it is the Lord I wish to serve.

Clip – scenes from the passion, the devil's temptation

It is not I that will build this temple. It is all mankind caring for one another and wanting to make a difference while they spend their lives enjoying all that GOD has given us.

GOD Heals His People

GOD is above passing the bucket, mankind is not. He who would be helped, help mankind, help your brother.

GOD's LEGACY TRUST – starts with one dollar

We have a bet
I bet GOD one dollar and servitude to show him that mankind can nurture one another and worthy of being saved.

Clip - The Bet – Trading Places - Servitude – Pirates of the Caribbean

What will GOD's LEGACY TRUST LLC spend its disbursements on?

I will give you this baby and he is not of your world, give him this, so that he will know his Father – Star Man

I can take him away, if you do not want this baby
Is this GOD's baby? – GOD's LEGACY TRUST LLC

We Report, You Decide – Fox News

When currency is dissolved. Will GOD's people help GOD's people? For the Joy that comes from Love.

Write this down in your hearts. Write it 50 times if need. I promise to GOD all that I am and will ever be. I will promote and honor all Gifts from GOD and go to great lengths to protect them. I would never betray what GOD is doing in my life by bringing in the devil to tear GOD's work down.

GOD's LEGACY TRUST LLC will disburse funds to separate entities, thus shielding itself from litigation.

People all around will beg for the opportunity to glorify GOD with their own gift of ....
Some will donate buildings that can be converted to health care centers. These centers will survive through LEGACY checks from all that have used them in life. "Move that bus" neighbors will join together to build these facilities. They will be televised for all to see the joy and gain encouragement to reach out and help your neighbor, in a way that will last an eternity. Let us be the generation known for saving the inheritance of GOD, not destroying it.

Leon Helmsley put her talents into the sand. The blessings she could have left the animals is mind boggling.

Whatever your passion is. You can leave a LEGACY check to them forever!!!

Just don't forget GOD. All he has ever requested was 10%. If you can't do it in life, analyze your lifestyle, then do it with your passing. You are each a building block to our future. If you do not use your talents. Ask GOD what you should do with them. He has a plan, do you?

What is GOD's plan?

I'm sane, I'm sane, I'm one of you. I am tempted, for I am merely a man. Do not glorify me. For all I do is for the Father.

GOD desires: Praise

World Peace – Miss Congeniality

Dreams – "If you build it, they will come"

Family – endless possibilities

Humanity – a cup of coffee a day

Basic Needs – Food, Water, Clothing, Shelter, Health

Care and FREEDOM!!!

He has shown you all how to pay for these things. Now he waits to see what we do with it.

Who am I Lord to bring this message to all of your people?

I am the lucky son of a GOD, born of this World, Asked, Cursed, Loved, Forgiven, Tempted and Chosen to deliver HIS message.

I understand now. I really do have Good News.

I have no audio of the father. He touches my heart. I have denied that temptation of earthly proof. I have FAITH.

It has been very difficult to have faith in GOD's people. I, that lie down in a bed of snakes, accept the consequences that I may be bitten from time to time. I accept the devil has his own entity and will forever tempt GOD's people. With the armor of the Lord GOD Almighty, the venom will have no effect.

I will sin again Father, It is how I am made – Broken

If I have thoughts of sinning against another of GOD's people. I will ask for forgiveness before harming any of your people. I will beg for forgiveness and receive it 7x70. My heart will be pure. My motives will be dictated by WWJD.

Your only begotten son left quite a good instruction manual. This is how life was intended to be.

GOD, please help your people help themselves by learning how to FISH.

Will GOD's plan teach people how to fish?

If a kid from a trailer park can be taught how to fend off evil aliens to save his world via a video game, I think GOD's children can be reprogrammed into a revived understanding of who we are, where we come from and who are Father is. We all are children of GOD and we each have a task to fulfill for the needs and betterment of our neighbors

George Bailey explains it best, your money is over here in her life and his money is over here in his house. – It's a Wonderful Life

GOD's money will be in all of our lives. GOD invests into his people. Who will be the one that returns GOD the most favor. The 5 talent man or the one talent man. He wishes to take your praise and heal the sick. Your businesses will thrive because GOD's LEGACY TRUST LLC will believe in your companies. Be honest with your stats, a financial statement tells a story. GOD's people deserve to know. GOD help anyone that betrays GOD's people. It is not a torment that I care to think of.

I hope Judas had a chance to ask for forgiveness, for he was only a pawn in the plan.

How will this create a foundation for GOD's temple?

I pray that you guide this humble servant in ways that touch everyone's heart. Guide me using our forefathers. Sample media to help me to present your message. You gave me the gift of Aletheia. Let me use it to glorify you Lord.

The foundation is GOD's people, it grows generation after generation. Read numbers if you want to be bored to tears or get the concept of compounded interest. The SWEAT, BLOOD and TEARS of our forefathers shall serve the Lord by serving ourselves.

Oh Lord, please give your humble servant the talents to convince mankind the only way to you is through Jesus Christ and his teachings delivered by him for you. Give me the wisdom to always do your will. Give me the gift of reacquainting your people to you. They are lost. With your grace that can be found.
Lord, please let me witness what you have built within me.

Clip – Treasure – Holes

I have stumbled so many times.

I still have something I would like to honor you with. It will be my gift to you my Father. So everyone can see all of my intentions were for your approval. It will not be a house of cedar, but of a … reminding all of your people the struggles of mankind. They will learn there of your Love for them and Heal on the inside. This will be a very special place that your children near and far will come to witness your Glory and Praise you. Everyone will leave with a New Name in Christ that only you and they know. It is how they will address you as Newborn Believers.

Will the people comprehend the magnitude of your gift Lord?

You my humble servant Nathan, you have cast out my nets, you may watch my Miracle. You may watch as my people find ways to mutually nurture one another when there is a shepherd to look after them. You do not possess the comprehension that would enable you to know the reach of your Lord. You will not live to see complete fulfillment, but you will see the fruits of your labor at my Direction and Timing

Lord,
I am so thankful for being given the opportunity to serve you and only you. You have your reasons for choosing me to spread the news. A used car salesman with an addictive personality. But I have faith and family. You blessed me with those. Give me the strength to do your will. Protect me from those that would slow your plan. I will cast your nets as far as your people will need. It will be up to them to harvest and tithe.

Your humble servant,
Nate
because I love you my Father

Will I have to contend with the disbelievers?

Yes, but remember I have buffers

What shall I tell them?

Bring my accusers forward worked pretty well for Jesus

But you allowed him to be crucified. Will I have to endure anything like that torment?

Sticks and stones may break your bones, but names will never hurt you. Words will, but you have your Faith and you have my WORD

This is my third attempt. Will you bless it this time?

I blessed it the first time, it was your impatience that got you in trouble. Always remember to wait on me hand and foot

In no way am I trying to claim your words as my own. I am answering my own questions with what you are putting on my heart.

I am fearful of you Father, but I revel in your Love.

How will I know who the genuine believers are?

You will recognize them by their Generosity of Time, Resources and Kindness to their Neighbor

Will this change the world?

Me, I can only hope so

Why did you make women so beautiful and so unpredictable?

Silly, it's the flavor of life. Be a humble man with a loving wife and you will find true happiness. You both shall revel in my Love

What should be done about gay marriage?

You know exactly where I stand on homosexuality. But if the Bach family can endure Arthur, then GOD's family can endure homosexuality. A marriage is between a man and a woman. If a couple wants to publicly announce their Love for one another and gain living rights, fine. But they know this is displeasing to Me and therefore they should not be able to subject a child to a perverted lifestyle. No adoptions

GOD Loves all homosexuals and FORGIVES. He is just displeased, as any Dad would be.

I feel like I am interviewing you Lord. But if this is my only chance, please enlighten me with valid questions. I feel like a walk on the beach. I love the beach. It is where I connect best with you. Please help me to remember your words, because I'm not carrying a notepad. My fingers hurt Lord. Let me rejoice this Labor Day weekend and finish my beer. LOL

September 6, 2009

Another Sunday will come and go Lord. I watched TV last night and instead of the ballgames I watched Prophecy on the History Channel. They predict "The End" to be in 2012. I guess I haven't seen that vision. My Vision is of HOPE and a PLAN that will work. They have not seen your Plan Father.

That is why they can only see the Destruction my Son

You're back!!!

I never left you

Just saw a woman walking a three-legged dog. The dog was happy and I know she loves that dog.

It is the sick that need your love. They already have mine and can revel in it any time they choose

It is Sunday. A day of rest. Must I write on the Sabbath?

Remember when Jesus answered the same question. But they were trying to trick him

Okay, put a little Miagi magic on my finger and let's write.

You are a silly man. You have my favor. My people relate to humor. They all want to be happy. But a joke is only short-lived. Happiness comes through the heart. A feeling of Joy, Peace, Fulfillment and Contentment that keeps you moving forward and enjoying life along the way

Will your people come to know you again?

As I told you before, your mind cannot comprehend my reach. As I promised, you will see the fruits of your labor at my Direction and Timing

As I look at the ocean, I am reminded of someone inventing a way for it to be converted to drinking water.

It has already been invented my son. Not limited to drinking water, but many resources. It is in the minds of the born and unborn. Their creativity is being suppressed

Are they square pegs trying to fit into round holes and society keeps telling them they are doing it all wrong?

Exactly, what are you doing Nathan, writing a book? LOL

Yep, I have a few people close to me that I want to take care of financially. But I will stick with giving you 90% and taking 10% for myself. No financial rewards could come close to the feeling of mission accomplished. I have faith in your people, my people. I am scared Lord. You spoke of the one that delivers your message being ill and in need of medical attention. If it is my time, take me Oh Lord. I beg of you to allow me health to deliver your message personally. You gave Solomon wisdom. I ask for Health Care for all Mankind. This is a humble request Lord.

It is starting to rain. Why do you plague us with disasters?

I EFFECT someone with everyone
They know my Wraith
Let those who would know ME appreciate
MY Strength, Forgiveness and LOVE

You always speak with a living word. You don't specify, why?

Because I speak in a different tongue to touch all who seek me. I touch their hearts in the manner I choose. Their minds do the searching

Oh, I've been meaning to ask you. Whatever happened to all those tapes that I sent Oprah? I am clueless to what is on them. You were speaking through me Lord. I have some I saved, but most went to her.

It matters not my son. You are still delivering my Gift. Keep up the good work

Thank you my Lord, my GOD, my Savior.

The rain clouds have disappeared and I am searching my brain what to ask you. Why do you not answer prayers?

I answer all prayers, you just might not like why and how I do it. And in your case, how long I will contemplate it

Damn right, I don't like what I have been through. But only now am I able to see how you were maturing me in faith with the pitfalls of life.

Why do you fill a man's head with desire enough to ruin their lives and the lives of others?

It is Restraint that shows their true character. Those without restraint shall answer to me. Jesus is a great defense attorney, but you must understand, I AM a …... GOD

I'm sorry my Lord. I cannot bear to think of you that way. I can only see the good.

I cannot share this with my family. I have worried them enough. I can only share with a few close friends, new close friends and those who don't know me.

How do you think Jesus felt? You can see the worry in her face. You can see the Love for her son. Your family already knows you. It is you that continue the Facade

I have found comfort in relying on you GOD.

I am always here for you to count on. I got your back

Had to brush that nasty taste out of my mouth. Now what was it you were saying? Oh yeah hygiene.

You must be clean before seeing the Lord. You must be kept always when not performing labor. You must report in to your assigned task for the betterment of your Brother. You already know how I feel about lazy through my son Jesus Christs teachings

I think you skipped over hygiene a little fast and went to work ethic. Can you expand on hygiene?

Do I need to!!! A Filthy Mind is a Filthy Body

Are We Clear – A Few Good Men

“CRYSTAL”

I have found people want to take care of their own and select groups and not be global.

Salvation starts within your family. Make your peace within your family. Then make your peace for your world. Your family is your foundation. Nathan my son, please don't question the reach of the GOD Almighty again

I will GOD, only when I seek your guidance. Forgive me for any doubts I have had. These are questions I must be able to answer for my accusers.

I watched the movie Green Mile last night. It was cool the way he shared the cornbread with the man who had asked for forgiveness and none with the unforgiven.

It is my plan to share the bread with everyone that will eat of me. You will have to carry those who would not

Hey, I wonder what those Pontiac Grand Am's are worth that Oprah Winfrey gave away. And I wonder what a LEGACY TRUST balance would have looked like today if the same money was invested, instead of a car purchase. Probably not all that great because the market took a shit. And people got hurt, got hurt real bad.

Nathan, ask me that same question 100 years from now. The answer depends on my people. All I have ever asked for is 10% and me, dammit. I want to give it back to you with interest

Me dammit huh. Is that why you commanded that we not take the Lord's name in vain. Because when it needs to make the most impact on your people, it is not watered down with use. We need to get this one don't we? I must admit, I did not tithe. I was not sure where to put what I have. I tried to give to your people on the street.

Nathan my son, my Wonderful Loving son. Do I need to educate you once again of the effects of Compounded Interest. It is not just Financial, it is Spiritual. Reflect on that commercial of doing good for someone else and it causes them to do something good for others. You will not live to see this. This will be a New Generation of GOD's People

I got my check. My great great great … grandfather must have been a pretty cool dude. I don't know how I would make ends meet right now if the subsidized healthcare that I receive now, was coming out of my check in taxes. Plus I'm getting a LEGACY check to boot. GOD Bless You Grandma and Grandpa.

"From the Estate of Nathan J. Isbell" – a humble servant of the Lord
"Endeavor to Persevere" - The Outlaw Josey Wales

I don't know about you, but I am fascinated by time capsules. What is revealed to future generations?

Here's one – we could leave such an astronomical debt that our country declares bankruptcy and all economies of the global world collapse.

I think I would prefer the Scooby Doo ending don't you. I'm going for a smoke break, stay tuned, as I think GOD is going to lay it out for you.

Hear Me My People

Dude, you gotta slow it down a bit. You are putting too much in my head at once.

Why do you slow me, when you have always hastened me?

I was frantic about your news Lord. I have learned to wait on you because your plan is bigger than anyone can comprehend at a glance.

That is why I desire an Earthly Entity through which I can Love my People. You will Build my Temple Nathan, with the Bricks of Mankind

Speaking of frantic. You spoke of future Prophets being suppressed. How can we fix that? I have a suggestion, but I haven't felt that on my heart yet. If whomsoever feel they have something on their heart that would be for the betterment of their neighbor, step forward – now call your neighbor. If whomsoever feel they have something on their heart that would be for the betterment of our world. Call me. Like a think tank.

I like it, but when they get really Confused, they call on me. Their Father

That was all me. I hope you approve father. Your grace leads my thoughts.

The plan must come my People, it is for the People, by the People and ME. So that you may continue your Praise and Love of ME. I give you the ANSWER

Disclaimer time: me is him, not me. Got to keep that one straight.

Hey remember that illustration I made of a perfect World and if $10 million were invested in 1985. I would challenge future generations to figure out how much that would be in their own time. Also the amount of lost time due to floundering looking for a way to honor our Creator. Thus denying a stimulus for our own survival. Go figure asking you for help is the Last Resort.

He gave me a great thought, then took it back for now. I have masterminded all kinds of ways to capitalize on your plan Father. Please forgive me.

You, who have Navigated your way through the Perpetuity Laws of your World, will be Blessed by the Splendor of MY Love, not of materialistic ideology

All I have ever wanted to do is please you Father.

Whatcha writing their George?

Science fiction stuff.

Get out of town. I never knew you had any creativity. Let me see.

I never show anyone my stories.

Why not?

They may not like them. They may laugh at me. – Back to the Future

What a shame – humble Nathan
Be quiet, they may want to give you a pill.

Let their Blood spill on the Blade of Ignorance.
Nathan you are my Sheath and I will draw my Sword from your Mouth, those that would not hear MY WORD shall PERISH

Hold up wait a minute, let me put some Scrooge in it. Are these the things that will happen or could happen. I prefer the Scooby Doo ending.

Charles Manson – what's up with that. I saw him on TV again this week. I want a place where people can go at their choosing to see how despicable mankind can become. I realize there will be a certain amount of erotic twisted thoughts. I hope and pray that you all are able to seek help before harming any of GOD's children. A discrete panic button will be available for you, you that need help. I don't think he needs any more media attention. If I care, I'll ask. Otherwise let the Lord have mercy on his soul and die.

Joke; a postman is retiring after 20 years of faithful service. The wife asked her husband what they should do for him. He replies, screw him, give him a dollar. She proceeds to screw him, gave him a dollar and cooked some breakfast for him. The postman is very thankful and asked the woman why? She said her husband told her to screw you, give you a dollar and the breakfast was my idea. LOL

LAUGH – what you know from funny

I have created your Earthly Entity with the paltry sum of one dollar. GOD LEGACY TRUST LLC. I will build this place. A place where people can seek guidance. That will be my gift to you my Lord. For all that wish to be healed, merely ask in your Holy name. Take what you need, leave what you don't. Always clean your plate and never be greedy with GOD's gift. By the way, GOD can be smoozed with a gift of Love. Now you know where to put it and receive it tenfold.

Father, I will deliver your word. I have no fear any longer.

Words and Music. They go together, without the Words there is no Music – Eddie and the Cruisers

September 7, 2009 Austin's Birthday

Ophiuchus – this is the name you have given me – your humble servant Nathan

Forgive me my Father for my impatience. I have hired Go Daddy to build your website. I do not possess the skills to do you justice. I pray that our web designer is a believer. I wanted to use my circle, but they were inept in their own skill sets, time and resources that would have ultimately only produced adequate results. This needs to be spectacular. With your direction, Lord speak through me your humble servant, to the web designer.

Everyone possesses a different set of Skills. Learn them, Love them and become Good at them. You will have my favor with a good work ethic. And then you can Praise ME for the Talents that I, your Father having given unto you. For I the Father, to give back to you Tenfold

Not to make a bad joke here, but isn't that a “Redistribution of Wealth”? -Nathan the Investor

LOL – yes it is. I want you to reinstate Birthrights. It is the Salvation for my People

In this book, can I use your words in red like Jesus has done in the Bible?

No, you may reverse print with red. My believers will put the red in themselves, if I reach their hearts

Is there a significance to red lettering?

Red represents the blood of my Son Jesus Christ, who believed in his brother and sister in Christ so much, he gave his own Life for yours. That is why you may reverse the red. For there are many who have come since. They cry out to their Heirs

My friend Brian told me his dying mother told him not to get caught up in life, but to live and enjoy his life. How can we live and enjoy our lives, if our responsibilities outweigh our income?

Live within your means and have a BACK UP PLAN!!! – Dad

I will loosen your yolk as I have done before. I will Heal my people, through my people. Your forefathers will subsidize your income and Praise ME

Tell me the story of Ophiuchus.

You read it online

Yeah, I know, I just wanted to get it in this book. I am very excited about my new Godly name. I have a different skill set from my predecessor Asclepius. He was a hands on guy. I want to hire someone with better skills than I and appreciate his skill set with compensation.

The lowest of the low will have your respect and my Blessing. Everyone touches everyone. All are touched by ME

Will the poor always be among us?

I don't know – Mr. Hand and Mr. Spicolli – Fast Times at Ridgemont High

I don't know, let's find out
one
two
three, CRUNCH
THREE – Tootsie Roll Owl

The Wise Old Owl predicts it will take three generations to grow GOD back into our World.

There are blades of grass and there are weeds. Check your own lawn for that answer, then check your neighbors

Abortion is a deep dark secret of mine Lord. (1st Wife) and I aborted one of your children. Only you know what that child has become. I beg for forgiveness from my unborn child and my GOD that I may be released from guilt for committing a sin. Thou shalt not commit MURDER. Lord, I ask you to put it on the hearts of young women to make good decisions. Young men are too horny. Whatever the consequences, touch her heart and allow her to choose the destiny that will forever be with her. It is her choice. Not one to be taken lightly.

Who will teach them how to make good decisions?

GOD &
Family – Churches – Schools – Mentors – Friends

I just busted a gut. You are a funny GOD and I love you. The Tootsie Roll Owl, Mr. Hand and Mr. Spicolli will now go down in history.

If anyone asks you a ridiculous question, refer them to the Owl or Mr. Spicolli

I was told that no question is ridiculous, is that true?

Yes and No
Think before you Speak
Think before you Correct or Humiliate
Be Gracious of Sincere Constructive Criticism from your Neighbor

DON'T BE – LITTLE !!!

Thank you GOD, that is something we should all keep in mind. I'm glad that I was laughing at myself.

I have been diagnosed with bipolar disorder. The only times of depression were when I couldn't be heard and made fun of or worried people. I think I am ADHD. Look at me, I am self diagnosing my illness. I definitely have the hyper part.

You are as I have made you. Your peers call it an illness. I call it a Gift. Ask any true mother. My children that have been suppressed or are suppressing others, will begin to allow their children to explore their creativity and encourage their efforts. It is through these efforts, that you will find comfort

Will I be asked a lot of questions about you and freeze like the frog cartoon Ribbit!

Let them read what is written for their own answers. I ask of no defense from you Nathan. Your sales skills will no longer be required

Cool, then I'll check you at the bar.

What about the people that won't participate?

My nets will catch all I will need to tend to the Well-Being of All

This place we spoke of as my gift to you Lord. It will heal many on the inside.

Is it not a gift from you. Should it not be a Surprise. The Gift that you would be given unto me, was put onto your heart by ME

Speaking of surprises Lord, is the Lord Jesus Christ coming to grace us with his presence again?

Are you Worthy to accept him this time? He is all around you now. He is the Holy Spirit. You have answered your own quandary. It's a Surprise

You know my daughter weighs heavily on my heart. I have not mentioned her much, because I have buried her in my heart. Am I the victim of parental alienation syndrome or a dad with shortcomings? I pray one day she will come back to me.

She is confused, but she will be Enlightened
I Will Be With You

This is a daunting task Lord.

I Will Be With You
This is my Body
This is my Blood
Do this in Remembrance of Me – Jesus

GOD's LEGACY TRUST LLC

Blessed are those that join in my miracle. Be hold my Mighty Hand

09 – 09 – 09
September 9, 2009
My thesis:

I remember seeing Sgt. York struggling with GOD and Country. The Bible pages were turned and he began to read "give unto Caesar what is Caesar's and give unto GOD what is GOD's" he didn't know the answer, but fought for his country until he did. He killed to save lives.

Please help me with this Lord. I need an opening statement that will encapsulate the essence of your message. What do you want me to tell your people about what you are directing me to do?

The LEGACY Will and TRUST gives you the opportunity to leave all that you are and will ever be, to your
Loved ones and Compassionate interests

GOD has put onto my heart a gift. He wishes me to share it with mankind. GOD desires an entity through which his people can praise him and he can bless them tenfold for all future generations for an eternity. – your humble servant Nathan

The Gift – The Lamb - GOD's LEGACY TRUST LLC

Explanation to web designer:

Please see the attached living TRUST and living will. This is the finished product of what this website is intended to achieve. I want people to be able to go on this site and establish themselves a Living Will and TRUST free of charge. After completion, they can print it out, get it notarized and file. It will also give them an opportunity to direct their inheritance and leave a LEGACY of their own. It will also give them an opportunity to square with GOD on the 10% they have been meaning to give him. Only now they know it will be directly for the good of their brothers.

GOD's LEGACY TRUST LLC:
Will reinvest 50% of its yield and disburse 50% for socialized healthcare. The government need not be involved. We have all been wondering how we were going to pay for healthcare for everyone. This is the answer.

As I compile all of the documents and write my intro for you, I realize that it is done. All I have to do is wait for the web designer to put your gift available for sale. Salvation. You want us to survive for your enjoyment. You've given us everything Lord. We can't screw it up. I am still amazed how you orchestrated my life to get to this point. Wow, what a ride. I would've never been able to write the story any better or near as good. I think your and my people are going to enjoy our book. Don't you? No wonder you needed a salesman.

I think that nasty old devil looked at the date wrong. It is 09 – 09 – 09 not 06 – 06 – 06. This is GOD's Day, for the Gift is Complete.

Now there,
How do you like me now?

I hope all are able to rebuke the temptations of the devil. I know I won't. But I know my father will forgive me. He says to remember the Laws of Moses and Jesus. They are our guide.

P. S.

somewhere in my reading, I saw that I am to interpret what 666 means. So here it goes, I was constantly looking for signs. Things that would indicate I was on the right path and not a psychopath. The more I looked for signs, the easier it was for me to find them. The devil is all around you and if you're looking for him, you're going to find him. He may even be on the front row. I saw all kinds of crap. It all made sense, at that time anyway. I guess I was searching for something credible and that made me pull the same kind of twist that Nostradamus drew from in Astrology. I don't know if there is anything to the dots that I have connected to who I am in Christ and my Purpose for GOD, but they are a collection of things that make you go Hmmm.... they could be further temptations from the devil. I'll let you be the judge. I know in my heart that I have fulfilled my Purpose for my GOD and earned my right to the Kingdom of Heaven. If the dots that I have connected, places me in the Constellation Ophiuchus as my place to dwell after my earthly flesh dies, I can dig it.

September 11, 2009

"LET'S ROLL"

I was so wrapped up in my own world, the one that mirrors the fiscal situation that our country is in. Although, I was personally not impacted by any of the Muslim Jihad terrorist, I have experienced the pain of loss through Hurricane Ivan. They say time heals all wounds. There is an exception. A wound that is not thoroughly cleaned out can appear to be healing, but will always fester up again and again. We didn't start this, but we Damn sure need to finish it.

The first time that I read through the Old Testament, I thought the total annihilation of cultures was to the extreme. I still do. That is the humanity and moral fiber of my being. The consequences of GOD's assigned task, had they not been carried out, would have been an everlasting battle with the descendents of the conquered. I pray this is not the only way to achieve World Peace. These terrorists and terrorist harboring countries, need to understand we do have a lot of cattle, not just a big hat. Our bite is as big as our bark. Our destiny is to live in peace. Anyone that doesn't want to play along "Gotta Get That Boom Boom Boom".

Ronald Reagan knew this principle all too well. You keep a bigger tank than the next guy on hand, so you don't have to use it.

Unfortunately, time has elapsed and this one appears to be healing. Unclean, infected and politically correct. The wound is festering to a boiling point with economics, politics, censorship, tea parties, war, perceived indecisiveness/weakness and the removal of the Constitution and GOD from our lives. Now I'm not a theologian, but this sounds an awful lot like what Revelations would look like.

This is a date in history that should never, ever become so politically correct that we forget who started all this. I pray for the families that lost loved ones on that horrific day.

I am sitting here on the balcony of my dream. I have dreamed of owning my own condo on the beach for a very long time. Now I have one and still longing for more. I understand that reaching the finish line is not important unless I can take everyone with me.

Seigar, you can do it. Climb that wall Seigar, climb it. – Officer and a Gentleman

The ocean rumbles today. I am waiting on you Lord. I pray that our new web designer is a believer and gets enthused with your plan.

I have been pondering your words of me not being able to comprehend your reach. You are right my Father. I cannot comprehend. Although I try and see the most glorious things coming from your gift, and it will work, but this is for an eternity and I can not envision your greatness for generations to come. I don't think your children will need another miracle, the miracle is you. And we will live GOD every day.

Think GOD –Oh GOD II

I am so anxious to get started. The website will be built finally. It was through a series of steps to get here. I reflect back on the last five years and shudder and rejoice. I have tried to pass this project onto someone smarter than me. It doesn't have anything to do with intelligence. I can hold my own in that department as well. It has to do with faith. What I saw was coming together for the third time, I knew that I could control my manic state. The euphoria was excellent. I have become educated about the symptoms, so now I can actually enjoy it without getting into trouble. What thoughts might you have, if you were convinced that GOD has put something on your heart and mind and kept you in a constant struggle to get it to his deaf people. It's hell. I desperately want to please my Father and my Dad. My dad plays it close to the vest. Maybe a little too close. Our relationship is strained and I wish I knew how to fix it. I feel I have disappointed him, but a half of $1 million will do that. That shows some true love, doesn't it. I think I would strangle Austin. LOL

Suicide – what do you think was on the mind of that man who leaped to his long agonizing death from the World Trade Center on September 11, 2001? What is on our minds, given much more options than that man. My ex-father-in-law spoke of suicide. He said he was scared to do it. He nearly did it with drinking and driving. He was lucky. I have thought of suicide on many occasions. My finances and family were crumbling. Just like George Bailey, I began to wonder if I'd never been born at all. I could not have made it through this Lord if it weren't for you. You caused it to happen and you could have helped me with the sting of divorce, but it was all in the script and what a Wonderful Script it is.

September 12, 2009

It's a jelly of the month club membership – Clark Griswold
That's the gift that keeps on giving – Eddie
– Christmas Vacation

Do you want to make a charitable donation to your favorite passion? Leave a LEGACY gift. It's the gift that keeps on giving.

I remember when I went to college. My dad put $10,000 into the market. I received approximately $100 a month which I would use as fun money at college.

One day, years ago on the golf course, I was working on getting life insurance and the idea came to me to leave this life benefit concept to my family.

2004 Hurricane Ivan forever changed my life. My journal detailing how GOD's LEGACY TRUST LLC was created.

Fox and Friends – just saw Karl Rove had some lunch to raise funds for the American Cancer Society. I think that is wonderful. If there was only a American Cancer Society

LEGACY TRUST fund. That would be the LEGACY gift that would keep on giving for an eternity. At the same time, put money into our economy and economies worldwide. The Lord's reach is endless.

If your passion is PETA. Give a LEGACY gift. I love that scene when the Pet Detective whacks the Monopoly guy and parades around using him as a wrap. I don't think if people saw what is entailed to get to the finished product of a fur coat, they would want one to fulfill a materialistic ideology.

I remember seeing a movie where Skinners found a family of raccoons with beautiful fur. They killed the family and hired Chinese women to sew the skins into garments. The women became possessed and sewed their own lips and nose together to suffocate. Weird movie. Is that what it will take before people realize, if it is food, then by all means take what you need, use all you take and not cause extinction. If you Kill GODs Creatures for pretentious status, then shame on you. You've been WARNED!!!

I am growing my hair out and I have a bed head this morning. I look like Peter Pan with a beard. I love that scene when the child pulls Peter's face back and says “Oh Peter, there you are”. It told me, Oh Peter you have lost your dreams, come back to your dreams – Hook

Have we unionized ourselves completely off the global competitive market. I think people would be grateful for a job right about now. What a shame these people worked their whole lives for a dream. Now it has turned to a nightmare. Where's my money? Our economy took a crap, sorry, oops. There is nothing wrong with our economy. It is the strongest in the world, but we are relying on borrowed money to support all the programs. We need to spend what we have. Our credit lines are exhausted. GOD's LEGACY TRUST LLC will heal his people. Caesar needs to pay back his debt to the World and invest into the World. So that one day everyone will receive the basic necessities of life. Food, water, shelter, health care and freedom!!! Caesar needs to teach leaders of the world how they can invest into their own economy and care for themselves. If they don't have a market. Let them invest in ours.

Damn, that was a good letter to the editor. I sent it to the Atlanta Journal, USA Today, New York Times and the Washington Post. I'll keep you posted.

This is the scroll with the Seven Seals. The Seven Seals are the Seven Deadly Sin's. The scroll is two-sided. The Vessel is LEGACY Will and TRUST and the Lamb is GOD's LEGACY TRUST LLC.

September 13, 2009

No word from anyone except Kim, who told me I was premature in sending this out. Maybe so, it's just very hard to contain my excitement. I have been here before. This time, I am controlled and patiently will wait on the Lord. Yes, I am back to hastening you again Lord.

September 15, 2009

Starting a business is a lot like planting a seed. You nurture it and reap the harvest. Why do we continually make charitable donations like seed to the birds. We must plant are charitable seeds, so that the birds can eat up its fruit for an Eternity.

September 16, 2009

I want to win my place in the constellation Ophiuchus like Phorbas did. I have created GOD an Earthly Entity through which he can bless his children. He put it on my heart.

These visions that you are putting on my heart Lord are wonderful. Is it possible? I know that it is, but will your people respond? These grandiose ideas are hard for anyone to understand, but YOU and I. It is fascinating to see you unfold the future before me.

I love how you made me love riddles.

Here's one:
There are two identical doors. One leads to heaven and the other to hell. There are two identical twins in the same room. One always lies and one always tells the truth and you are unaware which is which. You are allowed one question and one question only. What would your question be to ensure you choose the right door?

Which door is the one that you will choose? We make those choices every day.

Give up???

Knowing that I want to go to heaven, if you were I, what door would he (the other twin) choose?

They will both point to hell. LOL that's a good one.

I guess you can reverse the question or reverse your life if you want to go to hell. Then they would both point to heaven.

As I dance to have your way with me, I reflect on my hands the sign that I will give with both of them symbolizing two crosses and I am in the middle. Lord I am ready for my Crucifixion. Let my accusers come for me. This is all for you my Lord. Thank you for giving us this gift. Thank you Lord for giving me the tenacity to Endeavor to Persevere.

-Amen

Why have I not used amen in my journals before?

You had not seen my total vision Nathan. You will never see it in your lifetime. The use of Amen is a sign from me that there is closure in your purpose for Me

Thank you Lord, I am so ready for closure. To know that I will one day face you Lord. I am an open book to your people and to you Lord. All I am is in you.

Wouldn't that be a wonderful gesture to your neighbor. A wave with your hands symbolizing the cross. You can let everyone know that you have Jesus in your heart with a simple cheerful physical expression. I love it. The homosexuals can use the left-hand and the heterosexuals can use the right hand. Can't we all just get along – Rodney King.

Why can't we Lord?

Oh Lord, I think I opened a can of worms in my own life. I am a product of a discriminatory race and generation. I believe in race preservation.

Nathan my humble servant. When Jacob wagered with his father in law over the colors of the sheep, what happened? Did the spotted ones taste the same? There lies your answer

Yeah, I'm just not digging on the whole interracial scene. Maybe it has something to do with GOD being displeased with Solomon for marrying a different type of woman. It is very confusing, but I am sure that if there is love, the couple will be able to survive cultural boundaries, prejudice and family.

Love is the tie that binds – Mrs. Doubtfire

We should support their decision, because it is a brave one and not to be taken lightly. It is the cultural differences that need to be addressed. What does your community and you yourself exemplify? DO A PERSONAL, HONEST EXAMINATION. NEED A MIRROR?

Go freaking figure. White, black, yellow and green. If you are freaked up, you are freaked up. Unfortunately, there is a stigma that needs to be overcome. Can you do it? Reach high, reach to your GOD!!!

You want to hear some first-hand stories I have heard about the poor community. No, you don't. Your community must clean up and be Servants of the Lord. Then you shall receive the blessings of your Ancestors and your GOD.

Build, Build Yourself, Build Your Family, Build Your Community, Build Your Country

Then Build Your World – They are Your Neighbors

It is up to you. You hear me. Stoney, you in the garage. I'm talking to you. Be a betterment to your neighbor. Make a difference with your life. You know your purpose, learn from my experiences and bring your dreams to life to better the lives of everyone around you. Don't always expect monetary gain, for there is a much greater gratification to your own self worth that does not come from the almighty dollar.

Teacher says that every time a bell rings, an angel gets his wings.

That's right, That's right, Way to go Clarence. - It's a Wonderful Life

September 18, 2009

Cool T-shirt idea
Both arms extended with hands showing sign of the cross. Insert your pitcher in between, because Jesus is in all that except him.

Every LLC that accepts a dividend check from GOD's LEGACY TRUST LLC must provide full financial disclosure on public records.

This is funny. Last night I watched how a minnow of a fish was causing a drought to a land that feeds GOD's children out in California.

The reason it is funny, is a beach mouse protects GOD's Sanctuary. A beach mouse has held GOD's spot. LOL Well, I think it's funny.

September 19, 2009

The mighty beach mouse has held the Fort down. LOL Here's a novel thought. Get Marlin Perkins to relocate them. Get 'em Jim. LOL – Animal Kingdom

Hi Folks, Marlin Perkins here. Today we are relocating box turtles, but these waters have been known to be infested with bloodthirsty crocodiles. We are coming up on the bulk of the turtles now. Unfortunately for Jim, the bulk of the crocodiles as well. I have spotted the perfect turtle to relocate and Jim has entered the water. Get 'em Jim. Watch out for that...... oh well, did you get that on video? We'll submit it to Life's Most Dangerous Experiences. Some people will actually like watching this shit and pay to see it. That's screwed Up.

If we can relocate Native Americans, why can't we relocate GOD's creatures for the betterment of mankind. He loves us the most.

September 20, 2009

Went to my old church today. Hadn't been there in three years. Ever since the old man my ex-wife tried to befriend hit on her. Ouch, isn't it amazing how when GOD directs me to share his plan to the Minister, that he would be preaching on fulfilling your mission.

Mission accomplished

I am waiting now to see if your plan is accepted at your church by your spokesman. It really doesn't matter anymore. I have climbed this mountain before, I will shake the dust from my feet of any place that would not hear GOD's plan for our lives.

I was having some doubts again for the past couple of days and you gave me the sign I needed to strengthen myself through your Word.

It is through Jesus Christ my Lord and Savior, that I find strength to carry on and deliver his Gift.

The Masters Plan

October 17, 2009

You can be so much more
The bad stuff, is easier to believe. Have you ever noticed that – Pretty Woman

Stoney (Simba), you are more than you have become – the Lion King
Look harder, your Father is in you – Drafiki

Take Your Place
Endeavor to Persevere – Nathan – a humble servant of the Lord - "A Godly Man"

Have you ever indulged in marijuana?

I don't really see any relevance to my mission for GOD, but I'll come clean.

I have experimented with marijuana, but I didn't inhale and I never had sexual relations with that woman.
-Bill Clinton a.k.a. President William Jefferson Clinton

Nov 23, 2009

Here's a crazy idea. Since the Government has so much money, lets give everyone that completes a LEGACY Will and TRUST a $10000 LEGACY policy, so we at least will plant a seed for future generations. This will be a gift from your forefathers and country, so you don't have to wait for the 10 acres and a mule you think this country owes you.

Make something of your life.

Make a Difference.

Life is Grand.

It is what you make of it.

If this was a car deal, I would go out for a smoke while you think I am working real hard for you. Then I would come back and say Good News. GOD will throw in Everlasting Salvation in you will buy in TODAY!!! Sign right there on the dotted line, press hard, three copies.

CONGRATULATIONS!!! You've just become another wonderful brick in GOD's Temple. All of your Heirs will enjoy getting a LEGACY Check from your LLC for an eternity. Your Countrymen will thrive because of your insightful desire to leave the World a better place. Your favorite Charities and Passions can budget to help the masses. Your Creator can take his rightful place on this earth and

Heal His People...

How appropriate it is to finish this on

Thanks Giving Day

Happy Thanks Giving To All

May GOD Bless Us All

GODS LEGACY TRUST LLC
THE DREAM TEAM
GODS TREASURY

5 TALENT TEAM:
WARREN BUFFETT
BILL GATES

2 TALENT TEAM:
ROBERT KIYOSAKI
DONALD TRUMP

1 TALENT TEAM:
JIM CRAMER
JIM'S CHOICE

This is the talent that will make up GOD's Dream Team. A semi-annual progress report will reveal who will become the new 5, 2 and 1 talent team. May the best team prevail for the Glory of GOD.

Six positions and Six positions only. These positions will be passed along by the talent to the new talent of their choice. LEGACY

6 TALENTS
6 POSITIONS
6 MONTHS

666 He's all around you,
stop looking for him,
for you are sure to find
HIM

The bad stuff is easier to believe- Pretty Woman

Man, I am one hell of a salesman. I think I'll buy my own book. LOL

Thanks T.D. I like that line.

Mr. Lewis and I are going to build Ships. GREAT BIG SHIPS. (GOD's Financial ARK)

Stuckey (Stuckey in the Past), you and the rest of the ambulance chasers handle all the paperwork and keep us out of court.

It feels GOOD to build something, doesn't it?
- Pretty Woman

Why are we trained to tear down? GREED – POWER

Why do we always look to Caesar to fix us? He gladly will with plenty of corruption. He shackles the poor with perceived gifts and decimates the desire for a different life.

When Caesar controls Health Care, who will get the most bribes from the richest of the dying and heartbroken desperate?

The poor will always be among us. The rich will always come first in a corrupt system written by the rich, using the money and power of Caesar.

Maybe if Caesar's books were as transparent as GOD's, the people could decide if we want to spend tax dollars on researching the mating habits of the hobbledoodle worm. And if there are enough people that want it, let them start a TRUST for these worms and all of the other vicious Kenids. Why do we spend money on these bullshit programs when people are hurting Worldwide?

ANSWER: The LOVE of MONEY

Somebody is getting paid, you can bet your Ass and the Farm on that one.

GODS LEGACY TRUST LLC
THE VISION TEAM
GODS GOVERNMENT

LEPER PARTY '12

CO-PRESIDENTS:

NEWT GINGRICH
MITT ROMNEY

This is the talent that will make up GOD's Vision Team. If there is room on the ballot, let GOD have a shot.

You let a preacher into Carbon County?

Well, it wasn't as if we invited him.

When you bring Faith and Hope to a desperate group of people, they will dig in deeper than ever and nothing will break them.

-Pale Rider

OPHIUCHUS

ENDEAVOR TO PERSEVERE

First came my vision. It came at a very low time in my life, when I was actually coming up with business ideas to rectify my own fiscal mess. It evolved to my ultimate purpose. I pray that GOD does not put such a daunting task on your plate, as he did mine.

It has been a blessing and a curse to know exactly how GOD wants to deliver his people via a Gift and not have a voice strong enough to be heard. Believe me, I have tried to be heard.

Once I had the vision, it was a lot like the 1990 page health care bill. I shrank it to two pages to make it a lot easier to understand. This took a very long time. Five years.

I launched the website and Ta Da. Nothing. That is what sent me searching to find out who I am in Christ and if this truly is my purpose for him. I found a lot of dots that truly connected for me in my heart. They are way out their and could easily be misconstrued as opportunistic.

I am at the culmination stage of my purpose. Since I can not be heard, I am going to publish my book. It is a journal of the last five years of my life trying to interpret my vision and deliver GOD's Gift. It will be called - GOD's Last Will and Testament Revealed. Ophiuchus - Endeavor to Persevere.

This vision has completely destroyed my life, but GOD picked me up and created a much better one. The reason that I continue to persevere is, I can't get anyone to disprove my theory. My theory is: LEGACYWILLANDTRUST.com will create a propagating, everlasting, taxable income stream. GODS LEGACY TRUST LLC is the Earthly Entity through which GOD's people can praise him and he can bless all of mankind for an eternity.

My purpose for GOD is to reveal his Last Will and Testament. A Seven Sealed, Two-sided Scroll. The Seven Seals are the Seven

Deadly Sins. One side of the scroll is the Vessel (LEGACY WILL AND TRUST) and the other is the Lamb (GODS LEGACY TRUST LLC). On Judgment Day, I will be able to honestly say that I have exhausted all in my power to deliver his gift.

Hello,

My name is Nathan J. Isbell born Nov. 21, 1962 in Morocco, Africa. I believe I am Nethinim and possess the gift of Aletheia (unforget, TRUTH). This is my new name in Christ and my purpose for GOD.

OPHIUCHUS
ENDEAVOR TO PERSEVERE

Ophiuchus is a Constellation where a human named Asclepius (AKA Imhotep) dwells as a gift of guilt from the Greek GOD Zeus. Asclepius witnessed a snake bringing healing herbs to an ailing snake and this was the catalyst for his intensive study of medicine. Asclepius became so good at his GOD given talent, that he began to rob death. This angered Zeus and he killed Asclepius with a bolt of lightning and later gave him, for his good deeds, this Constellation to dwell.

The Medical profession adopted and modified the sign of Ophiuchus. They recognize that Asclepius was the first physician in existence. The staff represents the rod that was used to entice the "worm" to wrap itself around, much like a python would do to suffocate its prey, thus leaving the body and healing the sick. Of course the snakes represent the aforementioned.

Ophiuchus is also the 13th Zodiac sign that most are not aware exists. The irony to this is how ignorance plays a role in every day life. Because if it is not in our frame of reference, it does not exist and the arrogant, vocally robust continue to rule over GOD's people.

This is purely speculation on my part, but I interpret the Sun to be the Son of GOD and the wings to be the wings of angels. The galaxy of stars are our ancestors awaiting for man to figure out GOD's plan so they may join him in the Kingdom of Heaven. The snakes represent Temptation and Greed. The gold crown represents the crowns awarded to those who help fulfill GOD's destiny in their own lives by coming to the aid of others in need. The circle represents the many different talents that GOD has given us and the acknowledgment that every man with talents brings a lifetime of issues and experiences to the table. Through the wisdom of all TalentS should a verdict be met. The White Rose is the Rose of TRUTH and DEATH. Finally the large star represents the unity of all GOD's people praising Him and watching the miracle unfold before our eyes. The small cross is little 'ole me and YOU, the Helper.

The miracle is how GOD's Gift will "Fundamentally Transform" how we bequeath our life long efforts, thus creating a propagating, everlasting, taxable income stream for our world to become a better place. GOD's Global people should not be without food, water, shelter, health care and FREEDOM!!! This is not an entitlement, but the sweat from your ancestors brow. It is up to us not to become complacent when your LEGACY dictates your financial needs have been met. This is a place where all of your creative juices can begin to flow because you will have time to think of ways to better your neighbors life.

I have selected Ophiuchus to be the Logo / Insignia that shall represent GOD's Gift - GODS LEGACY TRUST LLC. To give all future generations inspiration that GOD dwells among us. He is in all hearts that would receive Him. It is GOD's desire to have an Earthly Entity through which he can bless his children. It is up to us what we make of it. GOD really does help those that help themselves and their neighbors.

Our lives begin to end the day we become silent about things that matter.

Martin Luther King Jr.

They are hard-hearted and stubborn people. But I am sending you to say to them,

"This is what the Sovereign LORD says"!

- Ezekiel 2: 4

I, Ophiuchus, AM WORTHY of Breaking the Seven Seals on the Scroll to reveal GOD's Last Will And Testament to all that would accept the Lord Jesus Christ, the only Man GOD to ever grace our humble existence by sacrificing his own life for the sins of Mankind. Father as directed, I have cast your net Globally. I can only pray that your people will heed your message and lavish in your Gift. The alternative is becoming increasingly evident by witnessing the extraction of YOU in our culture and lives. What would the world be like without GOD? NOT A Vision I wish to Envision.

I am merely the Messenger. Please don't shoot the Messenger. At least no one has shouted out “Blasphemy”, “Crucify Him”. That would suck. I'm blessed to live in a country to be able to do exactly what I am doing right now and I want future generations to enjoy those freedoms as well.

Always Respectfully Question Authority.

- Your Humble Servant Nathan
www.LEGACYWILLANDTRUST.com

LETTER TO:

BRIAN

Nov. 30, 2009

To: Brian Winkler
From: Nathan J. Isbell
Re: Executor of my Last Will and Testament

Make sure my Personal LEGACY is fulfilled.

PLEASE PUBLISH MY BOOK:

"GODS LAST WILL AND TESTAMENT REVEALED"
"OPHIUCHUS"
"ENDEAVOR TO PERSEVERE"

My password is **************.

Somewhere in the Bible I read to pray concerning my travels in the winter. I am a little afraid of this trip to Atlanta. Bill recently got his plane out of the shop. So to be overcautious, I am writing this letter to you.

Tell (2nd Wife) how I feel about her. Tell her I Love Her and always will. Tell her Good Luck on her book.

Brian, this is too important to not fulfill. Do this for me as a friend.

By me writing this letter to you, signifies that you know the very intimate details of my life. Good luck on your book.

I Love You My Friend,

Nate

INTERESTING REFERENCES

IRS DEPARTMENT OF THE TREASURY
INTERNAL REVENUE SERVICE
CINCINNATI OH 45999-0023

Date of this notice: 09-21-2009

Employer Identification Number:
[illegible]

Form: SS-4

Number of this notice: CP 575 G

For assistance you may call us at:
1-800-829-4933

IF YOU WRITE, ATTACH THE
STUB AT THE END OF THIS NOTICE.

GODS LEGACY TRUST LLC
NATHAN J ISBELL SOLE MBR
P O B 1371
GULF SHORES, AL 36547

WE ASSIGNED YOU AN EMPLOYER IDENTIFICATION NUMBER

Thank you for applying for an Employer Identification Number (EIN). We assigned you EIN 27-0961532. This EIN will identify you, your business accounts, tax returns, and documents, even if you have no employees. Please keep this notice in your permanent records.

When filing tax documents, payments, and related correspondence, it is very important that you use your EIN and complete name and address exactly as shown above. Any variation may cause a delay in processing, result in incorrect information in your account, or even cause you to be assigned more than one EIN. If the information is not correct as shown above, please make the correction using the attached tear off stub and return it to us.

A limited liability company (LLC) may file Form 8832, *Entity Classification Election*, and elect to be classified as an association taxable as a corporation. If the LLC is eligible to be treated as a corporation that meets certain tests and it will be electing S corporation status, it must timely file Form 2553, *Election by a Small Business Corporation*. The LLC will be treated as a corporation as of the effective date of the S corporation election and does not need to file Form 8832.

To obtain tax forms and publications, including those referenced in this notice, visit our Web site at www.irs.gov. If you do not have access to the Internet, call 1-800-829-3676 (TTY/TDD 1-800-829-4059) or visit your local IRS office.

IMPORTANT REMINDERS:

* Keep a copy of this notice in your permanent records. **This notice is issued only one time and the IRS will not be able to generate a duplicate copy for you.**

* Use this EIN and your name exactly as they appear at the top of this notice on all your federal tax forms.

* Refer to this EIN on your tax-related correspondence and documents.

If you have questions about your EIN, you can call us at the phone number or write to us at the address shown at the top of this notice. If you write, please tear off the stub at the bottom of this notice and send it along with your letter. If you do not need to write us, do not complete and return the stub. Thank you for your cooperation.

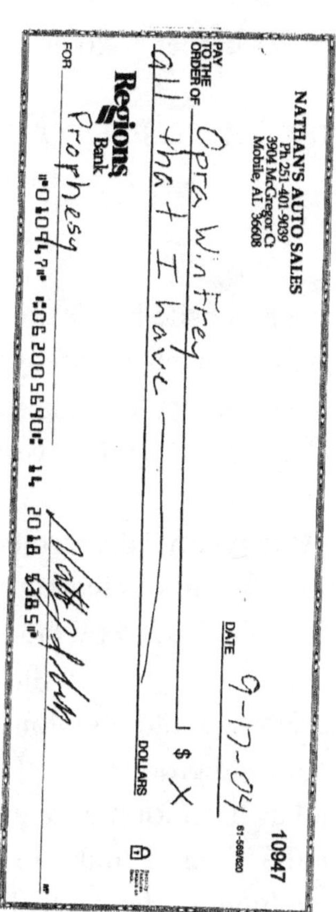

NATHAN'S AUTO SALES
Ph 251-401-9039
3904 McGregor Ct
Mobile, AL 36608

10947

61-569/620

DATE 9-17-04

PAY TO THE ORDER OF Opra Winfrey $ X

all that I have DOLLARS

Regions Bank

FOR Prophesy

December 3, 2009

PUBLISHING PROPOSAL

Dear Sirs,

I have reviewed your website briefly and I am lead to believe that the fees will be in excess of my limited cash resources. I have an appointment to speak with someone on Monday December 7th at 4:00 P. M. It is very important to me to get this message out.

If you do elect to take on my book project, is there anyway that I can pay you in Silver. I have recently purchased 500 ounces of Silver Eagle Coins sealed by the U. S. Mint. I am very concerned that our economy is in a Stealth Inflation and our currency is being debased into oblivion.

Somehow it is ironic and prophetic that it should come to this, but that is how it has been for me for awhile now. I am Cash Poor, but I have the Silver of Judas to offer up as "All that I have" to my Lord and Savior. May GOD Forgive him, for he was merely a Pawn in the "Script".

Thank You in advance for considering this Unique Proposal,

Nathan J. Isbell

The launchpad for new ideas

Fax this page
page 1

Inventor's Name: Nathan J. Isbell

File #: (if known) 1098263

Address: P.O. Box 1371

New Project Director:

City: GulfShores State: Al Zip: 36547

Home: ( )

Work: ( )

email: nathanjisbell@Yahoo.com

Cell:

Best time to call: any

Fax: ( )

CONFIDENTIAL SUBMISSION DOCUMENT

Invention Name: Legacy Trust

What is your idea?

What does it do?

How does it work?

Have you ever seen anything similar?

What makes your idea unique?

Who would buy your new product?

How much would you expect to pay for one?

How could your idea be marketed? (Retail Store, TV, Internet)

If you need more space attach pages to this document.

December 11, 2007

Nathan Isbell
P. O. Box 1371
Gulf Shores, AL 36547

RE: Provisional Patent Application
LegalZoom Order # 3143029

Dear Nathan Isbell:

Thank you for choosing LegalZoom!

We have prepared your Provisional Patent Application in accordance with your instructions, and filed it with the United States Patent and Trademark Office. Your filing date and time and application number are included on the Electronic Acknowledgement Receipt. This is your proof of submission. Please keep it in a safe place. Also enclosed with this letter is a printout of the electronic application that was filed.

A sample Non-Disclosure and Confidentiality Agreement is also included, which you can use to protect your invention whenever it's exposed to a third party such as a potential investor or manufacturer. The agreement requires those who sign it to take reasonable steps to safeguard the confidentiality of the information you share with them (note however that it is not a license). If you choose to use this agreement, please read it carefully to make sure you agree with all of its provisions and that it does not conflict with any other contracts you have or plan to have in place.

The Patent Office should contact you in approximately 6-12 weeks to confirm that your provisional patent application was received and filed. If you do not receive a response within this time period, please contact the Patent Office at 1-800-786-9199, using the application number provided above as your reference.

Please note that in order to claim the priority date of your provisional patent filing you have exactly 12 months to file a non-

provisional patent application. If you do not file a full patent application within this time, your provisional patent will expire.

Thank you again for choosing LegalZoom. We look forward to serving your legal document needs. If you have any questions concerning your filing, please contact us at customersupport@legalzoom.com.

Sincerely,

The LegalZoom Team

2

Legacy will and trust

DESCRIPTION

[Para 1] A legacy will and trust can:

- o Establish wills and trusts free of charge
- o Creates taxable, non-existing, never ending income stream
- o Provide instant taxation upon disbursement
- o Rebuild social security benefits
- o Reinstate birthrights with legacy checks
- o Create foundation for stock market because principle earmarked untouchable
- o Create personal legacy for all that participate
- o Fund socialized health care due to 100% of patented royalties paid by life insurance, financial planning and specialized will institutions to establish its own legacy trust
- o Create income for charities and research institutions without relying solely on donations or government funding
- o Feed the world and support Christian missions
- o Stop drug abuse with quarterly screening in order to qualify for a legacy check
- o Win the hearts of our global adversaries
- o Fund and mandate health care premiums for individual heirs
- o Provide buyers for the mandatory sellers of the 401k plans without panic of the absolute sell offs at age 70.5

- Provide assistance to single mothers
- Navigate through the perpetuity laws
- Answer the fiscal wake up tour challenge

[Para 2] Disclosure:

[Para 3] While the present invention has been described in terms of specific embodiments, it is to be understood that the invention is not limited to these disclosed embodiments, this invention may be embodied in many different forms and should not be construed as limited to the embodiments set forth herein; rather, these embodiments are provided by way of illustration only and so that this disclosure will be thorough, complete and will fully convey the full scope of the invention to those skilled in the art. Indeed, many modifications and other embodiments of the invention will come to mind of those skilled in the art to which this invention pertains, and which are intended to be and are covered by both this disclosure, the drawings and the claims.

[Para 4] Please understand that all items underlined fall under a scroll down process giving the individual the option of dollars, percentages and life insurance/financial institutions.

[Para 5] Rules and regulation for qualified recipients and/or charitable organizations

[Para 6] Each qualified recipient is entitled to an equal variable share of disbursements at age 18. (0,10,21,etc) note: best to allow time for interest to compound

[Para 7] Must register with investment broker 30 days prior to each birthday with proof of lineage and birth certificate

[Para 8] No liens may be attached

[Para 9] No back payments

[Para 10] Organizations that fail to register within 3 (1,2,etc) years will be deleted and proceeds to go into qualified recipient funds

[Para 11] If investment broker fees are excessive or the rate of return falls below 10 % (5,8,etc) for 2 (1,3,etc) years in the last 5 (1,2,3,etc) years a majority vote of qualified recipients may change investment brokers to a different legitimate broker under pre-set guidelines. tie no (yes) change

[Para 12] Minimum legacy check is $100 after fees and expenses, otherwise account will re-invest 100 % until this can occur

[Para 13] Only direct bloodline lineage qualifies, no extended families

[Para 14] Spouse of qualified recipients does (does not) qualify as my replacement upon my death.

[Para 15] Must register all births of your bloodline within first year. Income stream may not be sold for one lump sum. Both of these infractions risk losing your shares at a majority vote. Tie no (Yes).

[Para 16] Fund must have a positive yield or there will be no legacy check for that period

[Para 17] Click here if you agree to the terms of this document. This document supersedes all former documents.

[Para 18] Legacy will and trust website***

[Para 19] If this is for trust purposes only, proceed to step 3.

(1) Step 1: name of your life insurance company abc life (xyz life, etc.) if no current life insurance and you would like to contact an insurance company click here to go to life insurance link for free quote and consultation.

(2) Step 2: at the time of my death, please disburse 50 %(10, 20, 30, etc.) of my total death benefit as immediate cash funds to the following beneficiaries:

- o Spouse 50 % (breakdown of %'s default to equal 100%)
- o Child 25 %
- o Child 25 %
- o Special note: if a more complex will is needed, it is the responsibility and expense of the individual. Click here if you wish to proceed to specialized will planning link.

(3) Step 3: the remaining or total 50 % (default from step 2 or 100% if for trust purposes only) of total benefit is to be put in trust with ABC financial planners (xyz financial planners etc.)

(4) Step 4: name your LLC - it will appear on all legacy checks.

(5) From the estate of Nathan J. Isbell (allow creativity here)

Page 3 of 6

(6) Step 5: re-invest 50 %(10,20,30,etc) and disburse 50 %(default previous option equal 100%) of the monthly (quarterly, annually etc.) yield

(7) Step 6: legacy checks to be disbursed as follows:

- Qualified recipients 90 % (default to 100%)
- red cross 5 % (list all charitable institutions
- American cancer society 5 % as well as other–

specialized)

[Para 20] In closing, I respectfully request that the united states court of appeals and the united states patent and trademark office give special consideration to this invention as it will benefit us all and all future generations.

[Para 21] The time is now to find a solution to the fiscal wake up tour challenge that the US comptroller David Walker is desperately seeking. He states the "financial implosion" is on the horizon and the problem stems from "the power of compounding". Ironically, the solution is derived from the same statement. The answer is compounded interest.

[Para 22] After reading the USA today headlines dated 10/09/2007 I too was shocked to know the way our country is headed fiscally and I agree with Kathleen Casey-Kirschlings (1st baby boomer to reach retirement age) statement, I can't imagine what's going to happen with our children and our grandchildren," she says "they're not going to be able to retire." I pray this is not the legacy my generation leaves behind. By the year 2030. Two taxpayers to one retiree that did not plan well. Please take a quote from bishop T.D. jakes, "it is time for us to begin thinking gene rationally."

[Para 23] I feel it necessary to once again point out that 100% of the patented royalties (if approved) will be channeled to a legacy trust designed to implement socialized health care. This will cost the taxpayer nothing, help alleviate the tax burden and not interfere with private health care. As a U.S. navy brat, born in morocco, Africa having never served my country in the armed services, I hope this will pay my debt of service and be my legacy. I am proud to be an American.

[Para 24] May god bless America and the world,

What is claimed is:

[Claim 1] Upon death, the life insurance co. will have execution instructions to wire benefits to a legacy trust at whatever financial planner the policy holder has selected as trustee. The trustee will then disburse these benefits as the policy holder has imputed online or otherwise. These selections made at legacy.com or at the financial planners office, can be changed up until the time of death since no disbursements will occur until then. After the traditional immediate cash gratification and burial arrangements are taken care of, the remaining percentage of benefits will be placed into its own LLC. This LLC will be in the control of the trustee and invested into the U. S. stock exchange. After a 50% re-invest, the remaining 50% can be disbursed in the form of legacy checks. The disbursement and frequency of these checks will be dictated by the policyholder using the scroll down selection process on the website. One of the scrolls will ask for a corporate name. This corporate name will appear on all checks and can be anything non-vulgar the policyholder wants for all of his heirs to remember him by. All people that are direct descendants of policy holder are entitled to an equal variable share in the LLC at age? And all charitable organization is assigned a set percentage. The legacy trust website will be a simple easy to follow step by step process that will enable policyholders to convert their existing beneficiaries to a legacy trust online. The cost to the consumers will be $0 and they can establish a legacy trust of their own. Leaving their mark for an eternity. All financial planners will be listed on the scroll downs with links leaving the choice to the policyholder. The financial planning institutions will pay a royalty on my patent based on new conversions, sales and financial planning.

ABSTRACT

Enables every American to set up their own trust using their life insurance benefits and/or other assets. This trust will benefit all of the policyholder's heirs for an eternity.

EXAMPLE OF HOW THE LEGACY WILL AND TRUST CAN WORK IN A PERFECT WORLD WITH ILLUSTRATIVE BENEFITS

TOTAL BENEFIT - $10 MILLION
YEAR STARTED - 1985
ANNUAL INTEREST YIELDED – 10 %

YEAR -	BAL AFTER 5 % REINVEST -	TOTAL 5 % DISBURSED -	TAX 15 % -	CHARITIES 10 % -	HEIRS
1986	10500000	500000	75000	50000	375000
1987	11025000	551250	82687	55125	413437
1988	11576250	578812	86821	57881	434109
1989	12155062	607753	91163	60775	455815
1990	12762815	638140	95721	63814	478605
1991	13400955	670047	100507	67005	502535
1992	14071002	703550	105532	70355	527663
1993	14774552	738727	110809	73873	554045
1994	15513279	775663	116349	77566	581748
1995	16288942	814447	122167	81445	610835
1996	17103389	855169	128275	85517	641377
1997	17958558	897927	134689	89792	673446
1998	18856485	942824	141424	94282	707118
1999	19799309	989965	148495	98996	742474
2000	20789274	1039463	155919	103946	779598
RULE OF 78'S 78/5 = 15.6 YEARS					
OUR PRINCIPLE BALANCE HAS DOUBLED					
2001	21828737	1091436	163715	109144	818576
2002	22920173	1146008	171901	114601	859506
2003	24066181	1203309	180496	120331	902482
2004	25269490	1263474	189521	126347	947606
2005	26532964	1326648	198997	132665	994986
2006	27859612	1392980	208947	139298	1044735
2007	29252592	1462629	219394	146263	1096971
2008	30715221	1535761	230364	153576	1151821
		$21,725,982	$3,258,893	$2,172,597	$16,294,488

IF IN 1985 $10 MILLION WAS PUT INTO A LEGACY WILL AND TRUST, THE PRINCIPLE BALANCE WOULD BE $30,715,221. TOTAL DISBURSMENTS WOULD HAVE BEEN $21,715,982. THE GOVERNMENT WOULD HAVE COLLECTED $3,258,893 BASED ON A TAX RATE OF 15 %. CHARITIES $2,172,597 BASED ON 10% AND THE HEIRS WOULD HAVE SHARED A TOTAL OF $16,294,488. THE 2008 DISBURSEMENTS WOULD BE: GOVERNMENT $230,364 – CHARITIES $153,576 AND HEIRS $1,151,821.

Electronic Acknowledgement Receipt	
EFS ID:	2574548
Application Number:	61012841
International Application Number:	
Confirmation Number:	3271
Title of Invention:	Legacy will and trust
First Named Inventor/Applicant Name:	Nathan Jerome Isbell
Correspondence Address:	Nathan Isbell - P.O. Box 1371 - Gulf Shores AL 36547 US 251- nathanjisbell@yahoo.com
Filer:	Adam Thomas/Parthan Vishvanathan
Filer Authorized By:	Adam Thomas
Attorney Docket Number:	
Receipt Date:	11-DEC-2007
Filing Date:	
Time Stamp:	13:05:22
Application Type:	Provisional

Payment information:

Submitted with Payment	yes
Payment Type	Deposit Account
Payment was successfully received in RAM	$105

Hello Lauren,

This is the culmination of all my crazy ideas. I am sorry it took me five yrs to be able to tell you what they were in an understandable manner. I was not sure myself, I had to allow GOD time to mold me. I know you were scared and confused, I am deeply sorry for that. I had a turmoil inside of me that would not be settled. I was given a Gift and that was my purpose for GOD.

I Love and Miss you Lauren, I hope you still don't think your old man is crazy.

Your Loving Father,
Dad

nathanjisbell@yahoo.com
Ph 251-XXX-XXXX

AMEN

IN CLOSING

December 21, 2009

Dear Faithful Believers,

I pray that there are still at least 144,000 of you that have not discounted the Message that I bring, because of the manner and talents used to bring it to you. The Devil will try and use Ophiuchus to distract you from GOD's Plan. Keep your eye on the plan. ***The Vessel*** & ***The Lamb***

Scriptures do say that the Son of Man will return and His Kingdom and Government will be established for an eternity. If the Lord Jesus Christ has truly chosen me as His Messenger, I Pray that I have lived up to the task.

I am not going to run through the bible and show you scripture to try and make you believe, I've already determined that to be a waste of time. Each and everyone of you will have to make up your own mind whether you will be snatched up or left standing. You have a choice now that will be indefensible on Judgment day. You hold the fate for your ancestors and yourself.

I will offer you this. If Astrology is so bad, why does the bible say to look to the stars for guidance? The stars directed us to the birth place of Jesus. Who determined the Pentagram to be Satanic? Who checked their credentials? Could these same people that place themselves as Judge and Jury over our lives, resemble the same leaders that Crucified Jesus or maybe the ones that burned witches at the stake? Are we still so closed minded that we would continue to do Barbaric things because our frame of reference is limited?

Lord, I have delivered your Plan and fulfilled my Purpose for You. I pray for you to remove the scales from their eyes, so that they might see the Beauty and Magnitude of your Everlasting GODLY Love. - Your Faithful, Loving, Humble Servant Nathan

Amen

www.ingramcontent.com/pod-product-compliance
Lightning Source LLC
LaVergne TN
LVHW091035080826
845145LV00002B/509